Rajah
King of the Jungle

by
Balraj Khanna

Illustrations by Sean Victory

Mapin Publishing

Rajah

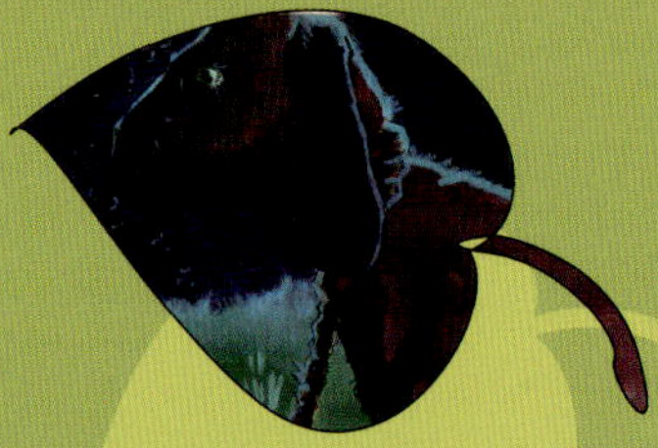
Bakri

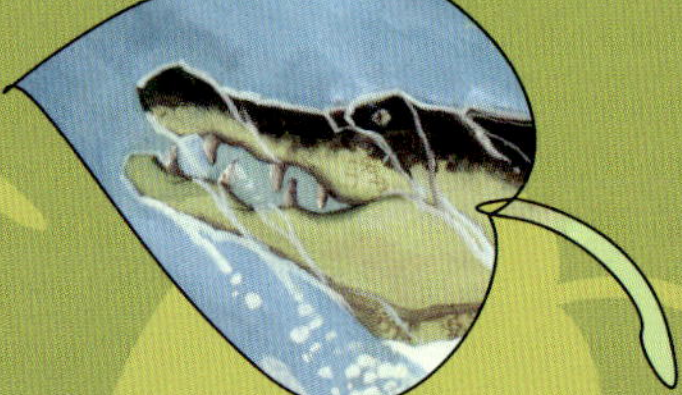
Magar

Bibi

with all my love to

DIMITRI
PIERRE
MIYUKI

Lil Squi

Mohan

Cheetal

Loombar

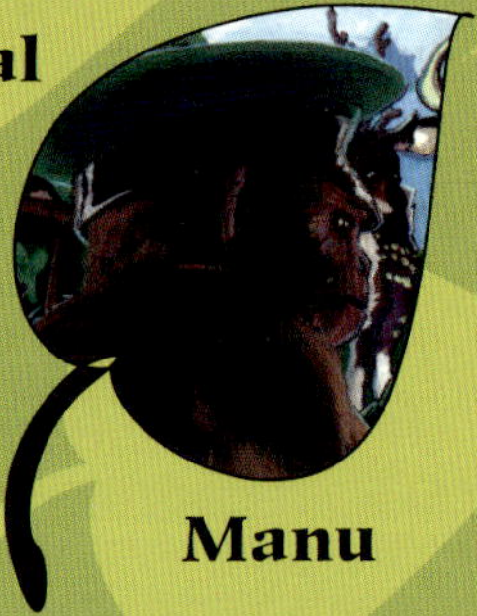
Manu

Banto

Tota

Nanda & Nandu

The Cast

Rajah – Tiger
Lil Squi – Squirrel
Mohan – Peacock
Bakri – Goat
Bibi – Cheetah
Cheetal – Deer
Magar – Crocodile
Ananta – King Cobra
Manu – Monkey
Khargosh – Hare
Banto – Female Bison
Bhaloo – Bear
Chuhi – Jungle Mouse
Hathi – Elephant
Hedgy – Hedgehog
Kiri – Ant
Kurma – Tortoise
Loombar – Fox
Mohini – Peahen
Nanda & Nandu – Bison
Panchchi Loag – Birds
Tota – Parrot
Chanda Mama – Moon
Surya – Sun

Contents

Rajah: King of the Jungle

Night fell swiftly in the jungle, coating it with jet black ink. Night always fell swiftly in the jungle. It was in the natural order of things.

On the surface, hiding secrets of Time itself, the jungle was as calm as calm can be. But underneath the calm, the jungle night pulsated with fear. It quivered with danger. Black as black can be, it was a theatre of suspense.

Rajah, the tiger, wearing his cloak of terrifying beauty, glided through his kingdom, the jungle, which had become an ocean of shadows.

His eyes, like burning embers, radiated ferocity that set the jungle alight with fear. And the moon, Chanda Mama, stole gracefully over Rajah's dazzling stripes, making the dark ones merge with the shadows and the fiery ones leap out to dance with his heavenly light.

Rajah roamed through the night and heard the distant hoot of the secretive owl, the laugh of the elusive hyena...and the metallic twang of some nameless creature.

Rajah saw the radiant Chanda Mama rise, becoming enormous as he hung above the treetops before sinking behind them.

Gradually, a blushful golden light rose from the other side, from across the river. The jungle breathed out a freshness which filled the hearts of all creatures with goodness. As dawn spread its warm glow, dewdrops shone like diamonds in a murmuring breeze – Mother Earth was under a spell.

Thirsty after his nocturnal walkabout, Rajah studied his ferocious features in the river water while he drank. He admired his own reflection and lapped up the deliciously cool nectar with a slow darting tongue. Having drunk his fill, Rajah turned his back on the river to face his jungle – an impenetrable mass of tangled trees, shrubs and shadows. But what did he see? – Two pinpoints of light, cold and hypnotizing. A shiver made his back ripple into an arc.

Ananta, the majestic Lord of the Underworld, sprang up from the thick undergrowth! Boldly, he spread out his supremely fearsome, hooded head inlaid with its mysterious mark.

If the mighty tiger set the jungle alight with fear, the King Cobra froze it with dread!

Rajah stopped in his tracks, inches away from Ananta.

'Move out of my way.'

'Move out of my way.'

The King of the Jungle and the Lord of the Underworld spoke to each other with their eyes, one pair radiating fire, the other emitting venom – there couldn't be two monarchs in the same dominion as there couldn't be two suns in the sky.

But neither creature gave way, both doing split-second calculations in their heads:

Ananta thought, *'If the tiger lifts his clawed paws to strike, I will wrap myself around him like lightning and inject my deadly venom in to his neck. He will die on the spot.'*

Rajah thought, *'Should the snake make the slightest attacking move...I will dispatch him to the next world with just one blow of my mighty right paw.'*

Neither the King of the Jungle nor the Lord of the Underworld budged an inch. Whoever retreated first would have admitted defeat. No junglebodies were around to witness the deadly confrontation. Only the jungle itself. It trembled with fear.

If they got into a fight, one of them would surely die. The jungle had to prevent such a fate befalling either.

Silently, it reminded the two of a certain ancient treaty.

'Rajah...!' called half the jungle behind him.

'Ananta...!' cried the other half.

This treaty had been made by their ancestors thousands of years ago, the inherited memory of which still throbbed in them. It bade Rajah and Ananta never to cross each other's paths. If perhaps they happened to, it was no sign of cowardice to withdraw and go their separate ways. But...

'Move out of my way,' the two adversaries spoke to each other with their eyes as if looks could kill! And the jungle cried:

'Rajah...!'

'Ananta...!'

The ancestral treaty throbbing in them, each creature dropped his gaze. Ananta glided away in a rhythmic serpentine movement as graceful as it was lyrical – a poem

in grass. And so indeed did Rajah, rustling into the stillness of the early morning jungle, becoming part of it.

The junglebodies did not measure age in years or months, but by seasons. Their calendar had five seasons: spring and summer, autumn and winter separated by the loveliest season of all, the season of the rains. Rajah and Ananta were both ten rains old, both in the prime of their lives. Never before this had their paths crossed and there was no reason to think it would ever again.

The tiger and the snake were not enemies. Nor was it hatred which divided them. An intuitive mutual fear forbade either to come in the way of the other. That fear had just saved one or perhaps both of them from certain death. But would it be the same next time?

Rajah and Ananta were members of the same extended jungle family, revered and feared by all. In the jungle, all creatures great and small co-existed side by side, never interfering in the affairs of others. Mother Jungle gave them all they needed. Their world was complete. Almost.

For there loomed a threat which presented itself in the shape of a being not of their world – humans. Humans were unlike any of the natural jungle folk. Humans were scheming and selfish. They killed for profit. In the eyes of the jungle family, humans were unnatural beings.

Humans were Rajah's main enemy just as they were Ananta's. Humans shot the tiger as a trophy. They caught the cobra so they could make money by displaying him.

Rajah decided to amble downriver to a grassy clearing on the banks, the junglebodies' common meeting ground. He hoped to find his old friend Magar, the giant crocodile, there. The two sometimes sat by the water's edge, talking of old times. Many, many rains older, Magar was a master storyteller. He had many tales of the humans who came to kill him or other junglebodies. Rajah's favourite stories were those in which they got eaten instead by Magar. Oh, how he loved the one in which Magar nearly swallowed a gun as well as a human! Rajah was just in the mood to hear it again. Every time Magar re-told a story, it sounded different – a fitting tribute to the storyteller's talent.

But Rajah's friend had company. The whole jungle had come to greet the new day! This happened very rarely.

Hundreds of Panchchi Loag – birds of all colours and feathers – were squabbling loudly in the top branches of the tall trees. This they did every morning – it was their way of welcoming the day. They were the first to spot Rajah.

In the river itself, Magar, the Master of the Waters was pondering the Morning Star. He was also trying to blow away a cloud-like cluster of mosquitoes that was hovering above his nose. At the riverbank, Hathi, the towering elephant, was playing with a massive log, turning it this way and that with his ivory tusks as if it were a rolling pin. Above them in a leafy fruit tree by the riverbank, Manu the monkey was making a racket, leaping from this branch to that for all to see. Down below, the spotted deer, Cheetal, was making his way leisurely to the river for a drink.

Further to the left, the turquoise kingfisher had just made an elegant dive. He was flying off with a quivering piece of shimmering silver in his long pointed beak.

Here on the right, Mohan the peacock was proudly showing off his colourful plumage to a besotted admirer, Mohini.

And while other jungle beings were doing all sorts of other jungle things, Giddar, the discursive jackal was engaged in a discussion of a serious nature with the pragmatic Loombar, the know-it-all fox. They had an attentive audience. Twitchy-nosed hare, Khargosh, and his wobbly-headed friend Kurma the tortoise listened raptly from the carpet of grass. As did the grey squirrel with three white stripes, Lil Squi; and the red-breasted green parrot with a yellow hooked beak, Tota. Up on a jacaranda tree, they listened with pricked ears.

Rajah rarely attended these riverside get-togethers. The sudden appearance of his burning striped hulk had an electrifying effect. All activity came to an abrupt end. Fear sent all hearts racing, all except those of his close friends, Magar and Hathi.

'Good morning, sire.' Magar and Hathi spoke in respectful unison, hoping to calm every junglebody.

Rajah acknowledged their greetings, nodding to other jungle beings. His manner – friendly – suggested he had come in peace.

But he had come only to see Magar. He turned his back on them.

'Don't turn your back on us like this, Majesty,' said Manu cheekily from his tree.

'Perhaps you don't think we are worthy of you,' squeaked tortoise Kurma from the ground.

'A king who thinks his subjects to be unworthy of him is not worthy of his subjects,' whispered Cheetal. Just as well it was a whisper.... If Rajah was quick to take offence, he was even quicker to react to it.

'That's being disrespectful to your king, Cheetal. You should be ashamed of yourself,' Rajah's best friend admonished Cheetal in a rough growl. Magar knew all there was to know about Rajah – proud and bombastic, yes, but never disdainful. That would be conduct unbecoming of a king. Yet while he was the most powerful of all, he was as vulnerable as any.

'Perhaps His Majesty is too proud and...' Manu added.

'Remember, pride comes before a fall,' interrupted Cheetal, looking sideways at Magar.

But Manu went on muttering: '...thinks he is too beautiful to mix with us humble jungle folk.'

'He is. Very beautiful,' Hathi said.

This pronouncement had a certain effect on the peacock. 'Everybody knows I am the beautifullestest,' cried the usually quiet Mohan. In a swift movement, he spread his feathers and completed the circle of his lustrous green-blue, turquoise, lapis lazuli magic. Then he danced around his paramour, Mohini. It was a dance of enchantment. The jungle was entranced.

'Wow!' it gasped. Even Rajah was impressed.

'Majesty is too proud of his coat, maybe?,' Manu said.

'And it is magnificent, cheeky monkey,' Magar said.

'Look at my exquisite plumage. Ever seen anything like it?' the peacock said with the smile of one in love with oneself. He was showing off. Someone had to put him in his place.

'Mohan, all you are is a bundle of vanity covered with fancy feathers,' said quick-witted Loombar, the fox. 'If your

feathers were not real, one would have thought you were going to a fancy dress party.'

'Or coming from one,' added twitchy-nosed Khargosh, looking in all directions all at once as he always did while speaking.

'We are talking about high-and-mighty Rajah. Not a silly-billy show-off like Mohan,' piped Kurma, wobbling his head.

Smiles broke out all around. Even Rajah couldn't suppress a smile. A tiger of few words at the best of times, he now felt at a loss about what to say.

'I am all you say I am. And I love you...'

'You have a funny way of showing it, though. Turning your back on us,' Manu said, hoping to make himself endearing.

'...And you love me.'

'Do we now?' chanted ten amused voices.

'We do! We do!' Magar and Hathi said, again in unison.

Rajah had said all he had to say.

'Good day, all.'

Proudly, Rajah padded away – an astonishing sight: rhythmic, beautiful, fearful. The King of the Jungle again became one with the jungle, indistinguishable from it. But the riverside repartee went on. It signalled a good beginning to the day.

While this strange meeting was going on in the jungle, it rained cats and dogs for a good hour up in the blue mountains nearby. Soon, the river which descended from the mountains and flowed through the jungle, swelled up and broke its banks, causing a flash flood. Most jungle creatures knew how to cope with floods – they came annually. But not all.

'I hate these floods. I hate them,' Rajah roared – he was half stuck in a muddy pool.

Manu in his tree by the riverbank saw and heard.

'Tut, tut! What about all that strength, Majesty?'

'Cheeky Manu. Are you being sarcastic? Sarcasm is the lowest form of wit, don't you know?'

'Me being sarcastic, Majesty? Never ever. You know me!'

The imperious tiger and the majestic cobra had never crossed each other's path till that morning and had not hoped to ever do so again. Yet here they were, face to face once more, due to an unseasonal change in the elements.

Rajah saw a swirling black line approach him with the same ease and grace with which it had disappeared in the grass a few hours earlier.

Even in the water, the King Cobra could raise himself!

Rajah was helpless. Unable to move, he could neither attack nor fend off an attack. He was totally disadvantaged and totally at Ananta's mercy!

Ananta came within striking distance.

'NO, ANANTA! NO!' screamed the Panchchi Loag from the sky.

'NO, ANANTA! NO! WE ARE FAMILY,' yelled Manu, Tota and Lil Squi from the trees, and Magar from the flood waters.

Hathi, the towering elephant, first heard their wail-like pleas. Then he saw.

'NO, ANANTA! NOOO...!' Hathi trumpeted, splashing his way like Magar with all speed to the scene of the King's death by poison.

About to wrap himself around the neck of the utterly helpless tiger and pierce it with his deadly fangs, the snake stopped. He heard that wail, that plea and he saw the gigantic Hathi and the great Magar racing towards him through the flood. The next instant, he rippled away out of sight in the muddy water.

Indescribable relief engulfed the jungle because its King had been saved. The water level of the river subsided just as suddenly as it had risen. The flood receded. The sun shone, drying the earth. The jungle was the jungle again, a self-contained world of its own.

But it was not Rajah's day.

Later that same afternoon, the scourge of the jungle appeared – two men with guns!

Again, the Panchchi Loag, flying in the sky now, were the first to catch sight of them.

'HUNTERS! HUNTERS!' they shrieked.

Alarmed, all junglebodies except Rajah rushed to the riverside for an urgent meeting.

It was not yet the season for shooting fowl and duck. Why then had the men come?

All jungle beings knew why. But no one dared say it.

'It's not true,' groaned Magar, as if in pain. 'It's not.'

'I am afraid it is true,' said Loombar, the know-it-all. He knew men. He understood their psychology. They were all the same – dangerous and greedy.

'Kill our Rajah just for his beautiful coat? No.' Tears poured down Magar's cheeks at the thought of the imminent shooting of his beloved friend.

'What will they do with it?' asked Lil Squi, the squirrel.

'Sell it for money,' Loombar replied.

Magar could not stop crying. His sobs rent their hearts.

'Oh, you and your famous tears, Magar!' Kurma, the tortoise chided him, 'Save them for another day when you eat a man.'

The birds in the sky spoke again, more urgently this time: 'HUNTERS! HUNTERS!' Then they flew out of sight.

'They are getting nearer and nearer,' Manu yelled from the top of a tall tree, gesticulating vigorously and scratching his belly, something he did when very alarmed.

An air of foreboding descended on the tranquil waterside. A long silence followed. The junglebodies were afraid of their king. But they didn't want him to be shot. Far from it. In their own way, they loved him just as Hathi and Magar had proclaimed that morning. Something had to be done and done *now*.

But what? No one knew where Rajah was. Finally, the crocodile addressed himself to the elephant.

'Hathi, you are not only the biggest in all the jungle, but also the wisest. We need your wise counsel. Speak.'

Like the others, Hathi was deeply moved by Magar's tears. Laden with melancholy, he looked at Manu up in the tree.

'Manu,' Hathi called out. 'Only you can help. Go leaping from tree to tree. Find Rajah. Warn him so that he can save himself from the bad men's bullets.'

'Go, Manu. Go,' they said in one voice. 'And Godspeed.'

'Now he will have to really, really love us,' said Lil Squi.

Manu sped away, swaying from branch to branch and tree to tree. Besides eating bananas, this was what he enjoyed most of all – swinging high in the trees. And what a wonderful sight it was, too, to see him cavorting so easily above them all! Manu and the trees were made for each other. When Manu swung through them, their branches complied with his every move. When he took a jump from one to another, they supply bent under his weight without breaking. Today, knowing that he was charged with a mission of life and death importance, they, too, urged him all speed.

But Manu was too late.

In a clearing deep in the jungle, Rajah lay on his side. The earlier encounters of the day were long forgotten – with danger always lurking behind every bush, junglebodies lived for the moment. Rajah was enjoying the warmth of the glorious autumn sun amidst the tall, golden grass. By instinct, he had taken the precaution to blend in with his surroundings. He had not a single worry to cloud his well-deserved rest.

One of the hunters was very tall, the other very short. The tall man had a long dangerous-looking scar across his face. His accomplice sported a moustache which curled menacingly up to his ears. He twirled its left tip as he spotted the tiger amidst the dense foliage, a defenceless twelve-foot-long striped shape. He nudged his partner-in-crime. The two could not believe their luck! Congratulating themselves, the hunters did the sums in their heads: How much would the skin fetch? And the bones, which would be ground up to make expensive potions?

Without disturbing a leaf or twig, they inched their way forward in silence. A hundred feet from their blissfully unaware prey, they stopped. Taking a deep breath, they put the butts of their rifles to their shoulders and took aim – the trophy was as good as theirs'!

'MAJESTY...!' screamed Manu hysterically from the last of the trees before the clearing.

Manu couldn't finish. Two deafening shots shook the jungle, causing it to explode into an orgy of noise – yells, cries and shrieks, sending the birds helter-skelter into the deep blue sky.

As dawn spread its golden-pink-golden wings over the jungle next morning, there was another get together. Junglebodies came from the farthest corners of the jungle. Every face wore the same expression, of gloom and doom. The news of yesterday's shooting had gone through the jungle like wildfire and the place was rife with rumour.

Some said the King was dead, others said he was badly wounded. Those junglebodies who feared the worst had tear-stained cheeks. Even the more hopeful ones had tears welling up.

With bated breath they had all come to ascertain the truth for themselves. The jungle had never known a morning to match this.

It never wanted to see another like it.

The truth was that due to Manu's timely screaming the hunter's attention was distracted for a split second and Rajah was known to run fast. He had escaped unhurt, though he was much humbled. The junglebodies had not been aware of his narrow escape. They wept tears of joy to see him at the riverside, as if waiting for them.

'My thanks to all you good folk for saving my life. A king gets the subjects he deserves.' Rajah laughed at his own remark as did the junglebodies.

'Who said Rajah was a tiger of few words? Why, our King can even make us laugh,' said Lil Squi, going near to sit on his back.

'Now who gave you the permission to walk all over me?'

There was loud laughter.

'The King saved by what, pray? A crocodile's tears! Now that's really something to write home about,' whispered wobbly-headed Kurma to his level-headed friend Khargosh, 'Manu would have gone anyway. He is a good-hearted monkey.'

By the riverbank, Hathi and Magar exchanged uneasy glances. They both had the same thought – Rajah was safe today, but what about tomorrow? They both knew that the jungle had not seen the last of the enemy. But they chose not to speak about it. It was not the right moment.

The sun soon began to shine and the Panchchi Loag started to squabble loudly. A swarm of white-green butterflies as thick as a monsoon cloud arrived from nowhere, fluttering about like the lashes of ten thousand twinkling eyes. The jungle began to vibrate with life. Everybody went away to start a new day – it was jungle-business as usual.

One and One make Eleven

Rajah never went near the enclave in the heart of the jungle where thorny bushes guarded a few mysterious holes in Mother Earth. No junglebody ever went there.

However, Rajah often had to go past this area, but he always bypassed this bush-packed white, sandy patch of earth. He kept a safe distance as a matter of course.

In the natural order of things, this place was out of bounds to the junglebodies. The jungle had unspoken rules and the junglebodies abided by them.

Rajah would usually have continued with his travels past the No-Go Zone late that afternoon. He was still some distance from it. But a strange sound coming from that place stopped him in his tracks. It made him curious because he thought he knew what it was. A master of camouflage and stealth, he stole through the dense foliage to take a look. And he proved to be right.

Inside the forbidden enclave, a man in loose white clothing sat cross-legged on the white earth. He was playing a pipe with a bulbous middle. An endless monotonous tune came out of the pipe. His two sons, also in white, stood by their father. They held two long and sturdy wooden sticks with wicked forked ends. Beside them lay two straw baskets complete with lids.

In an instant Rajah realized what it was all about. The musical crescendo built up and Rajah saw the most amazing sight he had ever beheld.

He saw Ananta and Lady Anantin pop their heads out of two holes next to each other in the earth. Then he saw them wriggle out and become still. They spread their hoods and began swaying from side to side.

The great cobra and his consort had been charmed!

The sons of the snake charmer made a move. They lifted their forked sticks to pin down the snakes and put them in their baskets. Completely under the spell of the hypnotic movement of the pipe, neither Ananta nor Anantin knew what was going to happen to them. They swayed on in a trance, as if intoxicated. The young men struck, pinning down their heads. Only then did the great snakes realize what had happened.

They struggled with all their strength and reptilian agility. But it was useless. Their heads were trapped between the forks and the white earth.

Rajah sprang into action and issued a huge, blood-curling roar.

'RAAAWWWR!'

Rajah roared again, advancing to pounce on the men. Petrified, father and sons ran for their lives, leaving behind their instruments of charm and entrapment.

With just two roars from his royal throat, the very throat that Ananta had decided against poisoning, Rajah had wiped his slate clean of debt. He kicked the forked sticks away.

Bushes have ears and soon the news of this remarkable incident was relayed to the entire jungle. In no time at all, every junglebody had heard about it.

The riverside was buzz-a-buzz.

This was unusual for the early evening. But today was special. Something or the other was always happening in the jungle. But there had never been anything to match today's drama on that white patch of jungle earth. This was what had made the riverside go buzz-a-buzz.

While junglebodies stood in small groups by the water's edge, away in a grassy field, there grazed a few neelgai (bison) unconcerned with the hustle-bustle near the river. But then the bison were always like that, politely keeping their distance. Today, two curious young males – best friends Nanda and Nandu – joined the junglebodies at the riverside.

Strangely, Giddar, the jackal, had no-one to talk to for once. Feeling left out, he began messing around with the helpless hedgehog, Hedgy. Hedgy had rolled up into a grey spiky ball. It was rather early for this night creature to be out and about, but Hedgy had impaled a berry on his spikes and was rather looking forward to eating it.

Suddenly, a number of junglebodies descended on Giddar.

'Stop harassing poor Hedgy,' the monkey rebuked the jackal.

'What's he done to you?' Cheetal was also disapproving.

'Why not pick on someone of your own size?' said Khargosh.

'Only having a little game with Hedgy. What's the matter with you people? Don't you like to play? You should, you know. Good for you, sport.'

'Did you hear that, Khargosh? Sport is good for you,' Manu said, raising his left eyebrow mischievously.

'Cheeky Manu. Anyway, early evening. Something to do.'

'Do something useful for a change, Giddar.'

'What, for instance?'

'For instance, go look for Lil Squi. Haven't seen her for a couple of days.'

'Anyone seen Lil Squi?' Hathi asked. He simply adored her.

'Must be gathering nuts. Autumn. It'll be winter before you know what's what,' said know-it-all Loombar. Usually, he could tell where any junglebody could be found at any time of the day or night. But not today.

'A bit early for that, isn't it? Where is the fidgety little thing?' Kurma sounded concerned – everybody loved Lil Squi.

'Something must be the matter with our Lil,' Khargosh said.

'It's unlike her to disappear for so long. Something is the matter with her.' Manu seemed really worried now.

'Go look for her then. Go, go, go!' Hathi said.

'On the double,' Manu replied.

Like Hathi, he, too, adored the little missy and often played with her. Their favourite game was chasing each other on open grassy spaces and up and down the tallest trees, leaping perilously from one to another. It was hugely exhilarating.

They hadn't even started the search when they heard the familiar shrieking from the sky:

'Hunters! Hunters!' – Panchchi Loag were homeward bound.

'Oh, no! Not again!' Manu was very, very surprised.

Magar and Hathi again exchanged glances – they were not surprised at all.

'We stopped them so convincingly only two days ago,' said Khargosh, the hare.

'We? What we? It was I who saved Rajah, putting my own life at risk.' Manu wanted credit to be given where credit was due, not misappropriated.

'Manu, our luminous star. What would we be without you?' Cheetal said with a wry smile.

'Extinguished.'

'But this time even you can't help Rajah.'

'I'll try to.'

'This time Rajah may not be that lucky.'

'You would like that, Cheetal,' Magar bellowed.

'You said that. Not me.'

Magar was distinctly annoyed with Cheetal. Manu took matters in his hands and changed the subject.

'I can't believe they are still after Rajah. Considering how I outsmarted them, they should never come here again. If they have any shame, that is.'

'My dear Manu, you know very well that the humans have no shame. They will do anything to get what they want. That's human psychology,' said Dr. Loombar, PhD in human psychology.

'I wish they would leave poor Rajah alone and come to me instead. I'll teach them a thing or two about psychology.' Magar said, licking his lips with his long tongue.

'Mind you don't swallow a gun this time,' Kurma said.

'If you talk to me like that, it's you I'll swallow, Kurma. But what are they up to today?' said Magar, looking at Hathi.

'Manu, ask the Panchchi Loag, will you?' Hathi said. Manu leaped up a tree and asked the birds.

'Actually, they are erecting a wooden structure – what looks like a 15-foot high watchtower,' came the reply.

'What?!' cried ten voices.

'To keep watch on us?' Manu asked, jumping down to the ground. 'Despicable. But typical! Mutants.'

'They are putting up a shooting post.'

'What on earth for?'

'To get Rajah once and for all. Go see for yourself, Manu. Here's a job for you.'

'Go, Manu, go,' urged several alarmed voices.

'Run like the wind and report back in double-quick time, Manu,' Magar said.

'Keep your wits about you and don't get shot,' piped Kurma. 'I'll be the first to miss you.'

'That'd be very nice of you, my dear Kurma. I'll do my best not to get shot. But don't get your neck in a twist if I do ...'

Manu loved such errands. They placed responsibility on his shoulders, gave him a sense of being useful to other jungle folk. So off he went, swinging merrily from tree to tree till he got to see what he had been sent to see. Peeping from the safety of the thick foliage, he saw the enemy, the same two hideous men of danger holding their rifles. They sat on a machchaan (a small platform) on top of the wooden tower they had erected. To the base of the tower was tethered a bakri (goat).

'My O my!' Manu mumbled, scratching his chest.

Having seen what he had been sent to see, Manu raced back to the jungle community, breathless with excitement.

'What did you see?' asked Magar.

'I saw, I saw, I saw ...'

'WHAT DID YOU SEE?' shouted all the assembled.

‘ ... I saw ... I saw our king’s favourite meal tied to the base of the shooting post and ...’ Manu could hardly talk.

‘And what? Speak. Are you monkey or human?’ Kurma said.

‘ ... And, and the two gun men at the top, would you believe? I’m afraid our Rajah has really had it this time. A bakri in the jungle? He’ll scent her from a mile and he won’t believe his luck. And that will be that.’

Everyone knew Rajah’s weaknesses, especially his most glaring – his craving for rare goat meat. Being domesticated, goats lived in the humans’ village at the edge of the jungle. Rajah used to steal one now and then. But when the villagers found out how their goats were disappearing, they had bought a gun, which they had fired without success at Rajah at least four times.

Again, the jungle community found itself in a sticky situation – what were they to do? Again, no-one knew where Rajah was. Again, Magar became all tearful. Manu was right. His friend had had it this time – no-one could keep having lucky escapes one after the other. And how many had Rajah had? Magar did not want to think about it. The writing was on every tree trunk around them – THE END.

‘These men are poachers. They should be put in jail,’ said the preening peacock, Mohan, the beautifullestest.

‘As I see it, it is quite simple,’ said Hathi, dependable as ever. ‘If we can’t keep the tiger away from the goat, we have to keep the goat away from the tiger.’

‘But how, Hathi?’ Magar asked.

Hathi shut his eyes for a minute to meditate. Then he curled his trunk and when he acted like that, everybody knew he had something up his trunk. But what could he do this time? The equation was simple. It was a death triangle: the goat, the tiger, the gunmen – a foregone conclusion.

‘Go, fetch Lil Squi, somebody.’ He raised his eyebrows right, left and centre.

‘Lil Squi!’ What could the little squirrel do?

‘Go and fetch her,’ Hathi said in a deep voice – it was more an order.

‘But what can that tiny little thing do?’

‘Only she can save Rajah this time. Go and find her. I’ll tell her what to do and no one else.’

'If only we knew where she was,' Mohan said.

'Look and you shall find.'

But they had no need to search. Lil Squi was behind Manu's tree right there, listening to them. She had great big dewdrops in her eyes.

'Ah! So here you are. But why are you crying?' asked Mohini most gently .

'Tell me, why are you crying, Lil Squi? Mohan said like a caring elder brother.

'Because I am afraid our Rajah has had it this time. Because I don't want him to die. Because I already miss him.'

'Oh!' they all said.

'Can I have a word in private, Lil?' said Hathi. He picked Lil Squi up most tenderly with his trunk and took her aside.

'Only you can save Rajah this time.'

'Me? How me? I am among the littlest in the whole jungle.'

'Yes, you. If you do what I say. And what I am going to say is dangerous. Very dangerous. But no harm will come to you if you are quick and careful. So listen up, brave Lil Squi.' Gravely, Hathi whispered his plan to her, adding, 'Top secret.'

Hathi's plan was simple, but bold. It was also very, very risky – one wrong move and.... It made Lil Squi shiver. She shook her head.

'Hathi, my friend, you are sending me to my death.'

'Do you want to save Rajah or not?'

The others, unable to stand the suspense of it all any longer, joined them. Lil Squi was still shaking her head.

'Please do what Hathi says, Lil Squi,' Manu said.

'Please,' they all said.

'Bow to the collective jungle will,' Magar begged.

Finally, Lil Squi did: 'All right. But just this once.'

That's brill, Lil. Really brill,' Manu said, tapping his left shoulder – an invitation for Lil to go and sit on it.

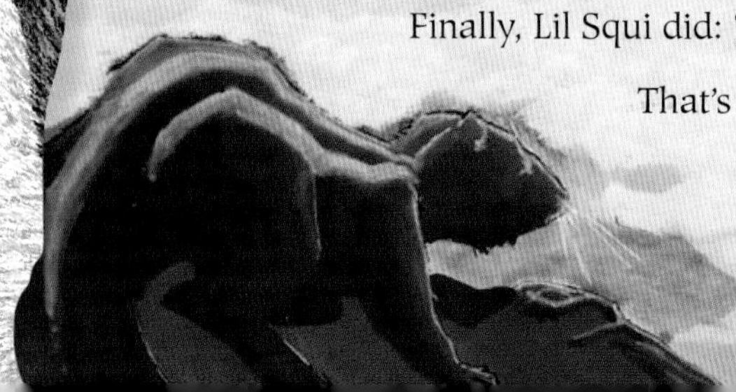

In the dark of the night, Lil Squi got ready to embark on her dangerous mission. Just then she heard a familiar sound from below her nest – Chuhi, the jungle mouse!

'I think I'd better come too.'

'You, Chuhi? I'm confounded. But why do you want to come?'

'To give you my moral support. One and one make eleven, you know!' said Chuhi, the brave jungle mouse.

'How do you know where I'm going?'

'I was right behind Hathi when he spoke to you. So I heard everything.'

'Oh, Chuhi. That was naughty of you – Hathi was talking to me in private.'

Lil Squi was only too glad of Chuhi's company. Together, they made their way stealthily to the scene of the anticipated crime – the merciless killing of the King of the Jungle. The two hunters were seated on their perch, guns in hand. On the ground below, the bakri was tied to a post, totally flabbergasted as to why she had been dragged all the way from her village to this godforsaken place of frightening darkness.

Then from nearby roared Rajah, for whom the stage was set for tragedy. It would happen any minute now, any minute – the scent of goat was irresistible.

Their hearts in their throats, Lil Squi and Chuhi appeared below the shooting tower – if the men saw, they would both be shot in cold blood. Heroically, Lil Squi set about her assigned task.

She started chewing through the rope which tied the bakri to the post. Although Chuhi could also chew, she let Lil Squi get on with it – her teeth so much sharper, she was so much faster.

There was rustling and similar soft noises. Only the two little junglebodies heard them. The unsuspecting Rajah was getting closer. In a matter of seconds, he would be there, and ...

Any second now, any second ...

It was a desperate race against time!

'Hurry, Lil Squi,' Chuhi whispered.

Lil Squi hurried. But there was only so much she could do.

'HURRY, LIL SQUI, HURRY!'

Chuhi was about to faint with worry. But she knew she couldn't allow that to happen – it would slow Lil Squi down. And she had come to support her.

'FOR GOD'S SAKE, HURRY!'

Lil Squi nibbled furiously. There were two strands left. She bit through the last one. The rope was cut, the bakri broke free and ran away into the black night.

It was not until dawn that the gunmen noticed the goat's absence. As they talked incredulously, curious Manu was peeping through the foliage again, taking stock of the situation.

'I say, where's our goat?

'It's gone. I can't believe it's gone. I had tied it securely with my own hands. Honest to God I did.'

'Look,' cried the first man, pointing to the foliage. 'It's the same monkey!'

'I bet he had something to do with the goat's disappearance.'

'SHOOT HIM.'

The man with the scarred face aimed his gun at Manu and:

BANG!

Later at the riverside the jungle community assembled to review the events of last night. Great praise was heaped on Lil Squi for her daring work and on Chuhi for her supporting role.

Everyone concluded that Rajah was still alive. And as if on queue, there was a roar and he arrived, looking supremely satisfied with himself.

'Guess what I had for dinner last night? Yum yum ...'

'You don't say?' Kurma said.

'I swear I did. And this time I didn't even have to go a-stealing from the human-village. The good goat ran straight into my open jaws.'

'Shame on you, Majesty! To think what we all went through to save your life yet again!' Kurma spoke without fear – he knew that even a king has sometime to be told to be humble.

'To save my life once again? How? Explain yourself.'

'And do you know who saved you this time, Sire? And that, too, at the expense of their own lives might I add?' Hathi said.

'Frankly, no.

'Of course you don't. Because you are always too self-obsessed. You never ever think of anyone else, do you?' Cheetal said what he had been longing to say for a very long time.

'But who saved me this time and from whom?'

'Little Missie, come forward,' said Loombar, looking at Lil Squi. He told Rajah the story of her bravery.

'A little thank-you would be quite in order, Sire,' Magar said to his friend of few words.

Magar was surprised when his friend spoke, that too like a wordsmith: 'Dear Magar, not a little thank-you. I shall sing our Lil's songs of praises in deeply felt gratitude. Lil Squi ...'

Lil Squi jumped on the royal back with total nonchalance – she had earned the right to do so.

'Also in order would be a little thank-you to this intrepid lady who kept me going by her unflinching support, placing her own life at risk.' Lil Squi pointed to Chuhi.

'Thank you, Chuhi. Thank you, my girl.'

'My girl!' Kurma whispered to Khargosh. 'My girl!'

This simple jungle politeness inspired old Hathi to say a few words relevant to jungle life, 'Nobody is too small, nor anyone too great. We are all equal in Mother Jungle's caring eye.'

While the others murmured, 'How true, how true!' Rajah said, 'Funny, I never thought about it like that in all my life.'

Simple, uncomplicated Rajah.

'But where is our Manu?' Rajah asked.

Suddenly, the entire jungle began to miss Manu:

'WHERE IS MANU? WHERE IS HE? IS HE ALL RIGHT?'

The branches of the voluminous bodhi tree overhead made a rustling noise and out leapt Manu.

Had Manu been shot?

Thank God, no, only grazed on the forehead by the bullet meant for Rajah. Rajah's name was not written on that bullet, nor Manu's. Manu had been stunned, though. But he didn't tumble or stumble. Bravely, he swung homeward, his limbs throbbing with a fear of an unknown kind – death.

'My battle with the bullet,' Manu began. 'I saw it coming and I ducked. But I was a tiny bit slow. See this?' Manu pointed to his forehead.

Everybody was moved:

'Ahhh!'

They thronged around Manu to see the spot where the bullet had grazed him.

'Next time around duck faster when you see a bullet coming,' Kurma said, 'Promise?'

'I will. But there won't be a next time,' Manu replied. Not even the greediest of men could be that determined.

Once again, Hathi and Magar exchanged uneasy glances.

Two Gentlemen of the Jungle

Far away from the riverside, in the tall, golden grass, Rajah lay spread out on his side, indulging in his favourite pastime – warming himself in the rays of the sun-god, Surya. He was breathing quickly but rhythmically. His eyes were closed but he was not sleeping.

Back at the riverside, Magar, half in and half out of water, appeared to be asleep. So, too, were Khargosh, Loombar, Giddar and the others in their selected spots. The whole jungle, it seemed, was sleepy. Even the ever-restless river breeze had ceased to dance. Above them all, the azure sky remained spotless with neither a cloud in sight, nor any Panchchi Loag.

Only Hathi, the great tusker, was wide awake. After a long and lazy mudbath, he was showering himself with vast quantities of cool river water.

It was quiet and peaceful. But their idyll was shattered by a deafening noise!

CRASH!

The branches of trees cracked angrily and two bison – best friends Nanda and Nandu – burst forth. Large and heavy, their coats were so black, they looked blue. Their curved horns interlocked in mortal combat. The earth shook with their weight and the half-asleep junglebodies were all rudely awakened.

The little night creature Hedgy, hurrying out of his hole, shrieked as loudly as he could, 'Save me! Save me! Save me!'

'What do we have here?' said Magar hoarsely, slapping the river with his mighty tail.

'Nanda and Nandu, would you believe?' Manu leapt from his tree and stationed himself next to his friend to watch.

Kurma, too, hurried there as fast as he could: 'There's a time and place for everything you know, lads.'

'Amazing. They're usually so quiet and gentlemanly, and the best of friends too. Whatever has come over them today?' Mohan said. It was truly amazing – the inseparable friends now joined in a battle to death, it seemed.

'I am astonished,' declared Giddar.

'Me, too,' said Khargosh.

'A sad spectacle. Never seen anything like it in all my life,' admitted Loombar.

'Neither have we,' said Panchchi Loag, startled out of the trees.

Hathi stopped showering himself and addressed all and sundry, 'But I have, being older than all of you. And I even know what it's all about.'

'Please, tell us then. Why are these two gentlemen of the jungle at loggerheads with each other?' Magar said. 'We are consumed with curiosity.'

'Well, that is because of a certain malady.'

'Then all we have to do is to find the cure,' said Magar.

Hathi shook his huge head.

'Alas, it's a malady for which there's no known cure.'

'But what's it called?'

'It's called jealousy.'

'JEALOUSY? What's that?' asked all present in one voice – no-one had ever heard of this.

'It's an affliction of the mind better known to mankind. But sometimes certain junglebodies also succumb to it.'

'What is the cause?'

'In the case of these foolish bison, it is right behind them.' Hathi pointed his ivory tusks to a lithesome female bison who had just appeared in sight some fifty yards away, grazing. She was breathtakingly beautiful. One to sing and dance about, to gore and be gored for. Even die for.

'But that's Banto. She's a cow, not a cause,' Cheetal said.

'She is both, I'm afraid,' Hathi said.

'Frankly, I do not understand,' Khargosh said shaking his head. 'Should we not separate Nanda and Nandu? They seem determined to damage each other. And if we don't pull them apart, they will. You'll see.'

'You'll do that at your own peril,' warned Loombar. 'When two bulls fight, only a fool would try to interfere.'

'These two are going to kill each other, you'll see. We are going to have murder in our midst, you'll see.'

'Khargosh, born pessimist, you always see the dark side of things,' said the born optimist, Manu.

'So what do we do? We have to do something. We can't just leave them like this.'

'That's exactly what we are going to do – leave them to their own devices,' Hathi muttered.

'What?!' Khargosh was shocked. 'Sometimes I really do not understand you, dear, wise Hathi.'

'Believe me. There's really nothing we can do. Well, not for the time being.'

Hathi went back to amusing himself in the water. The others also moved away, knowing that Hathi never said anything unless he had a good reason for saying it.

'Catch me if you can,' Lil Squi dared Manu and disappeared into the giant bodhi tree. Manu followed. He grabbed hold of one of the tree's countless hoary whiskers that reached down to the ground and gave chase, chattering to himself.

The short winter afternoon melted into early evening. A light mist rose up from the river, spreading over the riverbanks. Then, the sun-god Surya shed the last of his warming rays for the day.

'Poor Nanda. Poor Nandu,' Manu said. 'I feel sorry for them.'

'Me too. I wonder when they are going to stop. They will have to, when night falls,' Khargosh said.

'What about Banto? Why doesn't she do something to separate them? She should know how,' Cheetal said.

'Wonder what she is thinking.'

Then abruptly, the mist cleared. They saw Rajah come and go. He glanced at the warriors and turned his head away before disappearing.

Night fell swiftly, coating the jungle with black ink. The jungle felt the growing cold. Night deepened, bringing silence and night-jungle noises – the hoot of the owl, the

laugh of the hyena ... and the screech of the crickets. The silvery rays of Chanda Mama stole over those awesome stripes as Rajah toured his domain of rippling shadows, fearless and fearsome.

Most junglebodies slept in the safety of holes in the earth and tree trunks, in nests and on perches. But they could wake up astonishingly quickly with the slightest unfamiliar noise.

And by the riverside, huffing and puffing, the two young bulls still had their horns interlocked in a fight to death! They did not tire, nor did their anger show any sign of ending.

When Chanda Mama dipped down and was lost to the cold jungle, a golden blush rose from the other side. Gracefully, dawn came, bearing invisible moisture, to the delight of the earth, and filling every heart with that special goodness.

When the junglebodies woke up to the warm glow of sunrise, they found the two black-blue, blue-black bulls still there, huffing and puffing, issuing jets of vapour from nostrils widened in rage.

It was a pitiable spectacle.

'I don't believe it!' Manu yelled from his tree.

'It's got to stop. NOW!' Magar bellowed from below.

Hathi turned up. He had nothing to say, but they could see he was sad and sorry.

Then with pained faces other junglebodies also joined them.

'A whole day and night! Some fight!' Loombar couldn't believe his eyes. 'And what for? – Some unheard of malady called jealousy!'

'It's got to stop or it'll end in tragedy. We've got to do something.' Khargosh sounded desperate and his face showed it.

'But what?'

'I suggest we hold a Jungle Panchayat meeting. And I suggest we do it as soon as possible,' Magar said.

Magar's suggestion was eagerly accepted by all those present at the riverside. Word was sent out to others. Soon, junglebodies with anxious faces started arriving from every direction. Within half an hour, almost all of them had assembled there.

The Panchayat meeting could start now, with the wise old elephant in charge of proceedings. He hadn't yet opened his mouth when a quiet stirring in the grass made every junglebody at the riverside freeze.

That serpentine glide! That mesmerizing gaze!

Like Rajah, Ananta never attended riverside meetings. But today the jungle had a serious emergency on its hands. So he came, and it became clear straight away that he had come out of concern, otherwise he wouldn't have come at all. He coiled himself around the trunk of a very young neem tree next to a large clump of motia (jasmine) flower bushes in full bloom. Ananta flicked his tongue out since that was how snakes smelled and he loved the fragrance of the motia flowers.

'I cannot exaggerate the seriousness of the situation. Any ideas on how it can be resolved?' Hathi began.

Giddar said, 'If we had firecrackers, we could let off a few under Nanda and Nandu. That would separate them.'

'But we do not have firecrackers, Giddar.'

'If only we could talk them out of this thing called jealousy,' said Mohan.

'Wish we could, Mohan. But we can't,' Hathi said and turned towards Ananta. 'Any ideas, Ananta? You, more than anyone, know how the minds of all junglebodies work.'

'I have an idea, actually. But it's a tricky one.'

'Would you care to tell us what it is?'

'Get a handsome bull from another part of the jungle and let him charm the beauty away from ours'. The cause for their jealousy gone, these unfortunate fools are bound to come to their senses.'

'Brilliant. But how do we find the bull?'

'Send someone persuasive, someone with the gift of the gab.'

'But who, Lord of the Underworld?'

'Someone who's known to have the knack of a seasoned diplomat,' Ananta turned his head towards the wily fox and said, 'Loombar.'

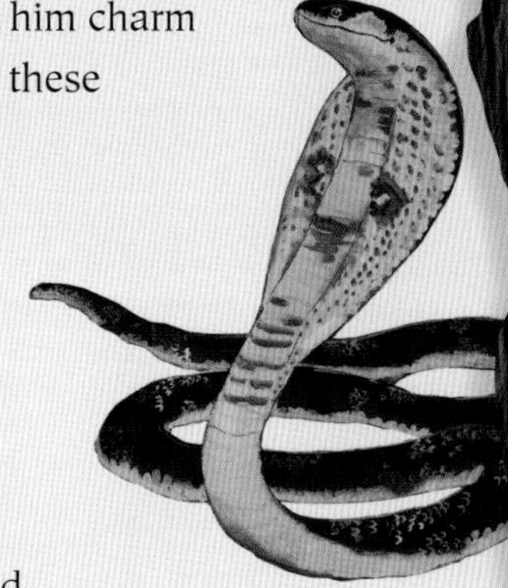

'Me? Why me?' Loombar protested.

'Because your tongue is smooth, like your fur. Because junglebodies listen to you when you speak. Because you are so well-travelled, you know where any junglebody can be found.'

'I knew my fur was smooth, but not that my tongue was too!'

'Go, Loombar. Take Messrs Cheetal, Giddar and Khargosh with you. Go as a proper Embassy with you as Ambassador.'

'Ananta, my tongue may be smooth, but yours is smoother by far, for you have talked me into it. Very astute, that. Very.'

Ananta did what no one present had ever see him do – smile.

It was a special, satisfied smile.

The meeting over, Ananta disappeared under the motia bushes to savour the scent of his favourite flower.

The afternoon came and a mellow sun bathed the jungle in golden light. But the junglebodies today were not able to enjoy their daily basking in the sun, for poor Nanda and Nandu were still joined in battle and the cow still stood grazing in a far corner, pretending she didn't know what was going on.

Hours later, as Hathi raised his trunk to shower himself with water, he noticed something in the distance which brought a smile to his deeply creased and deeply worried face.

'Ananta,' he called, knowing the great serpent to be still under the motia bushes, enjoying his favourite fragrance.

Ananta appeared – a long, black and glistening ripple in the late afternoon sun.

'Here they come, Ambassador Loombar and his Embassy.' Hathi was delighted. He let out a great spray from his trunk and heaved a loud sigh of relief.

'With a bull? Is he handsome?' Ananta asked. 'I can't see from down here. I only have a snake's-eye-view.' Ananta raised himself up two feet from the ground and spread his magnificent hood to take a look.

'But, of course. The cows will faint when they see him.'

'Now the question is how irresistible can the fellow make himself to our Banto?'

'That is the question.'

They did not have long to wait for their question to be answered.

The newcomer displayed no interest whatsoever in the duellers. He had eyes only for Banto. Loombar had lured him here to meet her. When Banto caught sight of him, her body underwent a sudden change. With melting eyes, she gave the new arrival a sidelong glance and then smiled at him.

'Well done, Loombar.'

'Brilliant, Loombar.'

Loombar tried to appear modest, 'A team effort, really.'

'Come, come. We know. And it's worked. Look.'

As the junglebodies watched, Banto and her new friend walked away together.

'What a fickle-minded cow!' quipped Kurma.

Mohan thought differently: 'It's a beautiful sight.'

'But the silly bison are still at it.' Loombar wasn't sure it had worked – the whole purpose of the exercise had been to separate them and end their fight.

'They won't be at it for long now,' Ananta said. He knew what would happen.

The very next minute, Nanda and Nandu disengaged. With eyes downcast, they moved away in opposite directions.

'Our happy, happy jungle,' Mohan said, dancing.

'Today, yes. God knows what's in store for it tomorrow,' Hathi said.

Look before You Leap

The events that unfolded proved that the wise old Hathi knew what he had been talking about.

Far from feeling ashamed of being fooled by simple jungle creatures, the greedy hunters had become more determined than ever.

They simply had to have the twelve-foot prize tiger. And this time they wanted him alive – a live tiger was worth a great deal more than a dead one. Having failed twice, thanks to that oaf of a monkey, they devised other means – tiger-proof and monkey-proof – to ensure complete success.

One fine afternoon, as the jungle converted itself into a theatre of a million shadows dancing like puppets and the junglebodies enjoyed a well-earned siesta, the two bad men returned. They were accompanied by four assistants who carried spades and axes. The jungle woke up at once. Noiselessly, it watched from shadowy hideouts invisible to the men.

At the orders of the hunters, the hired hands dug a trench ten feet deep and ten feet wide near the riverside. They covered it with light branches they had hacked from trees, with leaves and loose earth to make the ground look perfectly normal. Then the hunters and their men went away.

After a safe period of time, the junglebodies emerged from hiding. They came and stood around the covered pit, shaking their heads, unable to make head or tail of it all. It was indeed a very mysterious occurrence.

'Humans! Always up to something,' Manu said, scratching himself.

'Rather silly, wouldn't you say? First they dig a trench. Then they cover it up. Doesn't make sense,' said Khargosh.

'Whenever the humans do something, there's always a motive, usually nefarious.' Magar expressed his opinion with a shake of his massive tail.

'Why have they done what they have just done – make a deep hollow square under false earth?' asked, Chuhi, the jungle mouse. She knew all there was to know about subterranean cavities, passages and chambers, all made by nature for that was how Mother Earth was structured. But about this big hole...? Chuhi shook her little head...about this one she knew nothing.

As usual, Manu had an answer.

'I know why.'

Manu started jumping up and down on the false patch of earth, which puzzled the tortoise Kurma considerably.

'What on earth are you doing, may I ask? Up to your usual monkey business, no doubt,' Kurma said.

'I'm testing the ground, if you want to know. Well, it is strong enough to support me. Cheetal, dear Cheetal, be good enough to walk here a bit...'

The spotted deer obliged. Nimbly, he trotted over the length and breadth of the covered ditch a couple of times, taking an odd jump like Manu. He, too, was puzzled, though.

'...The surface can take the deer's weight, too,' Manu continued, thoughtfully.

'But it won't withstand the weight of a heavier body, I'm sure. I think I have begun to understand,' Chuhi said, jumping – suddenly, she had seen a ray of light.

'Me, too.' The peacock Mohan nodded his delicate head. 'The bad men want to trap our Hathi.'

'No, silly. They trap elephants differently,' Manu said. 'With the help of a tame elephant, they herd wild ones into an impregnable fortress made of logs, and voila!' Manu snapped his fingers.

'The tiger! They are after Rajah, our king!' Magar put two and two together. If the giant crocodile had fingers, he too would have snapped them.

'Spot on.'

So once again, the crocodile urged the monkey to go and warn the tiger. Manu, eager as ever to please his friends and to make himself useful, took off at top speed like he had the other day, swinging through greenery. He looked here and there – in this glade and that thicket – and finally found Rajah in a remote part of the jungle reclining amongst reeds that were exactly the same colour as his covetable coat. His fearsome eyes were closed. Rajah was so well camouflaged that anyone other than Manu would have missed him and gone back to report the failure of the mission.

'Majesty, wake up.'

But Rajah was not asleep. He opened his eyes. First he yawned, then he roared. The sight of his teeth – long, sharp and ferocious – instinctively sent shivers down Manu's spine in spite of Rajah's recent declaration of love for every junglebody.

'I was treating myself to a sweet little rest. You'd better have something important to say to justify your intrusion.'

'They are after you again.'

'What? Who?'

'The humans.'

'Men with guns?'

'No. Men with spades this time.'

'I better eat a couple of them. That will teach them a lesson. But why are they after me so persistently?'

'They are after you for your beauty, obviously.'

'Ironic, this, don't you think? That beauty should become the cause of the destruction of the junglebody who wears it. But they can't get me with spades alone? I am too strong for them. You know that, Manu.'

'Come and see for yourself what they've done to get you – *alive*, I might add.'

Rajah rose to his feet majestically. He stretched himself to his fullest length – twelve long fearsome feet – and shrugged his priceless coat. It opened Manu's eyes, the tiger's unique beauty at once became vividly apparent to him as it never had before! In that instant, Manu understood the bad men's lust for his coat – greedy men would never leave the tiger alone. It struck Manu as a tragedy.

Overhead, Surya, the sun, smiled benignly on their lush jungle. And a gentle breeze whispered through it sweetly.

'All right, then, Manu. Let's go and see what they have done to get me and then let's do something appropriate about it.'

Manu leapt from tree to tree – his swiftest mode of travelling – Rajah followed on the ground – jumping over bushes and ditches, which was how he covered jungle distances when in a hurry. In due course, they arrived at the covered pit where other junglebodies awaited them.

'Men? I see no men.'

'Majesty, they've gone to come back later when they've got you where they want you.'

'And what have they done to get me this time. I see nothing untoward.'

'Majesty, look ...'

But was Rajah listening? As usual, he wasn't.

'They have run away. They were frightened that I would pounce on them like this...'

To demonstrate what he meant, the impulsive Rajah roared frighteningly, took a long leap forward and landed on the false ground.

CRASH!

The false earth caved in and Rajah fell through it to the bottom of the pit. He roared and roared angrily, shaking heaven and earth.

'Dear, oh, dear!' said Khargosh, his nose twitching uncontrollably at the drama.

'I can't believe it!' cried Mohan.

'A king, more than anyone else, should think before he acts,' mumbled Kurma, popping his neck out of his shell.

'Dear, oh, dear!'

'Stop oh-dearing and do something!' Magar admonished them and everybody stopped talking.

The big question was:

WHAT COULD THEY DO?

The crafty men had got what they wanted – the tiger at the bottom of a pit, to be carted away and sold to a zoo. Silence prevailed, only shattered by Rajah's helpless roars.

'None of the present company can get him out of *there*. I'm afraid our king has had it this time,' Cheetal spoke at last, not entirely unhappy at the bizarre turn of events.

Old Magar disagreed strongly – he was not going to leave his old friend in the lurch. He was going to do everything in his power to have him brought out safely.

'But there is someone who can,' he said, quietly, looking towards Manu.

'I know who,' the quick-thinking Manu snapped his fingers.

'He who plays with logs.'

'Bravo. Go and fetch him then.'

Manu leapt away enthusiastically. All those present stood around the pit helplessly, watching as Rajah roared and roared.

In another part of the jungle, Loombar the fox heard the roars and guessed that the tiger was trapped in the bad men's net. He ran and came to see.

'Trouble?' he inquired from the assembly.

'Double trouble,' Khargosh said.

'Don't just stand and stare. Do something!' Rajah roared.

'Chuhi,' Kurma said to the jungle mouse. 'Be good enough to dig a tunnel for His Majesty.'

'Not the time for your wisecracks, Mr Wobble-Wobble.' Then Rajah turned to the others peering at him. 'Get me out of here before bad men come and cart me away. Hurry, do you hear?'

'Patience. Patience,' Khargosh said.

'Is that all you can say?'

What else was there to say? Or do, for that matter? But, understandably, the impulsive, simple and bombastic Rajah was not in the mood, or the situation, to appreciate that. He was trapped in a pit with ten-feet high walls he could not scale, however high he jumped or leapt, and he jumped

and leapt as high as his mighty leg muscles permitted. His fate was sealed.

He roared and roared in hopeless desperation, poor Rajah. Time passed. Slowly and painfully, it passed.

Then: 'Look! Look! Look!' Tota shouted excitedly from a tree, flapping his beautiful green wings.

The giant Hathi came trundling along towards them.

He held a long log between his tusks and trunk. On his back sat Manu, his head held high and looking grand like a maharajah. It was a spectacular sight. It brought hope when there had been none.

'Make way. Make way for the rescue operation,' Manu shouted, his voice full of lordly urgency.

Just then, Panchchi Loag in the sky shrieked:

'HUNTERS! HUNTERS! HUNTERS!'

Having heard the tiger's incessant roaring, the hunters knew they had him trapped. They hurried to the scene with their hired hands now pulling a great sturdy cage on wheels.

Their scheming and planning had paid off – success at last, sweet success – the quarry was caught.

The hunters appeared in the distance with the men with the cage on wheels to take the trapped tiger away.

'Hurry! Hurry!' cried those present at the pit.

'Don't panic,' Hathi said with complete composure of which only he was capable.

'The hunters are getting closer,' yelled the junglebodies as one voice. 'HURRY! HURRY!'

Now it was the hunters who couldn't make head or tail of what they beheld – a wild elephant carrying a log with a monkey on his back, and all those animals! Even a crocodile – what on earth was he doing there among them, the monster of muddy waters?

The sight was indeed astonishing. The men had never seen anything like it. They were dumbfounded. Whenever in the past they came to the jungle to hunt, all the animals ran away as fast as their legs could carry them, and made themselves invisible and unavailable as targets. But today? Today was becoming unforgettable. Today was too good to be true.

'Shoot them! We have the tiger trapped. Shoot them all,' shouted the leader of the expedition, the man with the badly scarred face and the villainous look.

So tense was the moment that the jungle beings at the pit were mesmerized by it! They had forgotten the danger they were in, forgotten the threat of immediate and certain death! They just stood around the man-made ditch, about to be slaughtered en masse.

Coming well within shooting range, the two hunters put the butts of their guns to their shoulders menacingly, yet no one at the pit budged an inch.

The massacre was about to commence.

Meanwhile, Rajah roared. His last moment had come. If anything was to save him, it had to come from the heavens above and from nowhere else.

And it came. It came just then.

Something from the sky fell on the men.

The Panchchi Loag had alighted on their heads and shoulders flapping their wings in front of their faces and confusing them and completely obscuring their vision. The timing was perfect. The Panchchi Loag had done the jungle proud!

'Oh, evil birds!' cried the man with the absurd moustache.

'Not birds! They are flying monsters!' said the other.

While the men struggled with the birds, Hathi hurriedly lowered the log into the pit. Freedom came quickly and Rajah vanished with the junglebodies, muttering: 'Thank you all again. Where would I be without you?'

'Look before you leap next time, Sire,' chirped cheeky Manu, jumping from one low branch of a tree to another. For once he missed, fell flat on the ground and burst out laughing despite the gravity of the situation.

'You, too, Manu,' replied Rajah, disappearing.

Poach the Poachers

Sunlight had trouble filtering through the dense mass of leaves to reach the jungle floor carpeted with moss and grass. Even when it reached the ground, it fell in countless, ever-changing patterns due to the jungle breeze. Surya, the sun, seemed to be playing a game of hide and seek. Manu looked up through his tree – now Surya was there and now he was not, now he was blinding and now was not. When Manu shut his eyes, he could still see the sun – a pink-orange glow – and feel Surya's warmth inside his eyes. It was fun. It was fascinating.

While Manu was employed in this game of sparkle and shine with Surya, a sizzling debate was taking place under his tree. The topic being discussed was the same old one – humans. Why couldn't they leave the junglebodies alone?

'We don't bother them, why do they bother us? In fact, they will do anything to harm us,' said Cheetal, his big eyes bashful, his white spots leaping out in sunlight.

'What I don't understand is why? WHY?' Loombar said.

'It's in their nature.'

'When it's not our flesh, it's our skin they want.'

'In my case, my tusks and my bones even,' Hathi said.

'In mine, my feathers,' Mohan said.

'Even poor little me, for my shell,' Kurma said, 'to make elegant things. They think it's good taste.'

'Ah, but most humans don't have any taste.' Mohan knew a great deal about taste and those who had it and those who didn't.

'Humans will shoot me, declare my meat a delicacy and serve it to princes and princesses,' Cheetal went on. 'Am I to be flattered? No, thank you very much, I am not.'

'Quite right too,' Loombar said. 'And what do they have to offer us? Nothing. NOT A THING.'

'We neither want their skin nor their bones.'

'We never want to see them in our jungle. Only out.'

'Humans break laws to kill me for my tusks,' Hathi said.

'What do they do with them, I wonder?' Giddar asked.

'They sell them illegally to unscrupulous traders for large sums of money, of course. They dispose off my bones similarly. To make ornamental things and small statues, sometimes of me! Believe it or not. Imagine a hundred little Hathis made of me!'

Manu, listening quietly from his tree until now, took a neat jump and landed in the middle of the assembly, exclaiming, 'I think it's atrocious! I think it's barbaric!'

Kurma popped his head out of his shell again. 'If you want my opinion, Manu, it is worse. What they call inhuman should really be called inanimal.'

'Governments should form anti-poaching squads and poach the poachers to stop this sordid practice.'

'They should without further delay,' growled Magar, picturing the grisly treatment he would receive if he ever had the misfortune of falling into human hands. 'But will they? Of course, they won't. Humans are the most insensitive of all living beings. Why I cry after I have eaten one, I don't know. Maybe I am too soft.'

'Humans are selfish, greedy and cruel,' Mohan said. 'Thank God I am not one of them.'

'Gives me the creeps just to think of it,' Manu said.

While this was going on at the riverside, from another part of the jungle, the fiercely determined hunters were making their way towards the junglebodies yet again, this time with strange-looking equipment, metal contraptions of some sort.

Their mission – to capture as many junglebodies as possible, especially that oaf of a monkey. Tota, who had been flying around trees looking for ripe fruit, saw them and heard them discuss their plans. He flew back as fast as he could to where he knew his friends were gathered. Tota swooped down and perched on Manu's shoulder, startling him.

'Stop your idle talk and prepare,' he squawked urgently.

'Prepare? Prepare for what?'

'It's them again, those shameless hunters and their men. And this time they want all of you.'

'WHAT?!' cried all present.

'And you in particular, Manu, to teach you a lesson for messing up their plans.'

'How do you know?'

'I eavesdropped on them. And today they've come with metal traps. You put one foot on one and SNAP! and you won't have a leg to stand on. You'd be a goner, Manu.'

'Our poor Manu,' Mohan said.

'And to make sure they get all of you, they've laid many such traps. They've gone away now. But they'll be back at first light tomorrow to "a massive bag", as they put it.'

'This is serious, very serious – all of us goners, all!' muttered Magar, his voice heavy with the weight of the approaching tragedy.

'But you'll be all right, my dear croc, you who inhabit the water,' said Loombar, the clever fox.

'You, too, Hathi, dear friend. Your feet are too big for the traps,' Tota said. 'And yours, Kurma, are too small, your weight too light. So you also have nothing to worry about.'

'Ah, then there are some advantages in being either too great or too small. How interesting!' Kurma said, looking sideways at old Hathi.

In spite of Tota's pointing out that Hathi would be safe from the traps, Hathi's face, gnarled like the bark of the bodhi tree, became contorted – he worried for his light-footed friends. 'Those abominable men.'

'What can we do? Migrate to another jungle, the one across the water?' Manu said, more fearful than the others – the men had a particular score to settle with him, it seemed.

'Not fair, that. We'd be invading the other junglebodies' home,' Hathi said.

'How would you like it if they turned up in ours tomorrow?' Loombar said.

'Food for thought. What do you suggest then?'

Loombar, cool and shrewd as ever, paused for a while before replying.

'You may think it utterly absurd, but since you ask, I think we have to beat the humans at their own game.'

'You must be joking. Beat the humans at their own game? Why, they are the cleverest beings in all existence, the most cunning, too. We can't beat them.' Khargosh shook his head. He knew what he was talking about.

'That's just what I mean – we can.'

'How, Loombar?'

'Let's find the traps, study their mechanism and then ingeniously render them harmless.'

'BUT HOW?'

'Let's locate them first. Tota will point them out to us from the air.'

'And I will do what I can on the ground,' Kurma said.

The meeting broke up. With the exception of Magar, who couldn't travel far on land, all the others followed Tota. He went flying from tree to tree.

'There...there's one!'

They surrounded the dreaded object, their foreheads furrowed and their eyes filled with profound mistrust.

'So this is the instrument of my capture!' Cheetal said, leaning his head forward to study the two pieces of steel held together with a spring – but keeping his feet well away.

'Looks harmless enough, though,' Khargosh said, keeping his distance.

'Appearances, my dear friend, are often deceptive,' Loombar remarked.

'How does it work?' Manu asked the question which was burning the tip of every tongue.

'Pick up that stick, Manu, and give it a poke,' Loombar suggested.

Manu picked up a stick from the ground and poked the thing with the spring.

There was a loud cracking noise as the trap shut on the piece of wood. Tight, irretrievably tight. 'See?'

'My O my!' Manu tried very hard to pull the stick out of the trap, but he couldn't. 'Had it been my foot, I would have been...'

'A goner.'

'My O my!'

Tota came and perched on Manu's shoulder reassuringly, saying, 'There isn't a human who can catch our Manu.'

'What's the next step?' Cheetal asked, conscious of the fact that had it been his foot, he, too, would have been a goner and on his way to a prince's kitchen.

'We have rendered this one useless. Let's deal similarly with the others. But how many are there? Did you count, flying angel?'

'That I didn't, Loombar, I'm afraid,' Tota replied.

'Oh, dear. Not very good, that.'

'Tota, you do your best and locate as many as you can,' Hathi said. 'I'll do my best and trample the jungle floor to smash those you miss.'

'Good idea,' Tota said, flapping away from Manu's shoulder.

Tota went flying from tree to tree, looking out.

'There's one...'

Manu poked a stick in it and... SNAP!

'There's another...' SNAP!

'...And another...' SNAP!

Manu poked sticks in the traps and they became harmless. At the same time, Hathi went around thumping the ground with his enormous feet, crushing one here and another there. Without them noticing it, dusk had advanced on them, bathing the jungle in a mellow golden light which brought a sharp chill to the air. The day was done.

'We've done a good day's work, I would say. Wouldn't you?' Hathi said to Loombar.

'I would, too.'

'Who's been the hero of the day then?' Hathi said, smiling benevolently like a patriarch.

'Loombar, good old Loombar,' all present cried in unison.

'Come. Come. I did what any self-respecting fox would have done under the circumstances. It was a team effort really.'

Loombar blushed – he could be ever so humble at times.

'Shall we not then call it a day?' Hathi asked the hero of the day.

'I think we may,' Loombar said and as he said that, tragedy struck with the speed of light. He stepped on an undetected metal object and SNAP! A heart-rending scream tore through the evening air.

'OH, NO!' groaned Hathi. 'OH, NO!'

'OUR POOR LOOMBAR!' cried Manu, scratching himself – every junglebody's heart was on fire.

It was tragic, it was ironic, it was unfair – the one who had the genius to thwart the men's machinations had become its undeserving victim. 'There is no justice in this world.'

Loombar screamed in agony. What was worse, nobody knew what they could do to help. Tomorrow, the bad men would come back, shoot him, skin him and sell his fur to furriers in the city. If only someone strong could unclamp the trap to release his foot. Although Hathi had the strength, it was not enough. Dexterity was also required. Strong pressure had to be applied simultaneously on the two pieces of steel to compress the spring enough in order to release Loombar's foot. Poor Loombar. He really seemed to be a goner.

'Wait a minute,' Manu cried, clicking his fingers. 'Magar. Magar can do it. He's got jaws.'

But the river was quite some distance from the scene of tragedy. The Lord of the Waters would never be able to crawl on land this far. Nor could Loombar walk. He wailed. His cries brought all other junglebodies to his side; except for Rajah, who was at the other end of the jungle, stalking prey. They formed a circle around Loombar.

'Let us not lose our presence of mind,' Hathi said. 'We'll take Loombar to the river.' Hathi picked up Loombar in his massive trunk as gently as if he were a new-born baby.

Solemnly, in a long procession the like of which had not been seen in their living memory, they proceeded towards the river.

Cheetal and Khargosh ran on before them to alert Magar.

A question cast dark shadows in their mind – what if Magar had gone fishing upstream or down?

But in fact Magar was waiting for them eagerly to hear the results of their all-important outing.

They surrounded Magar. Gently, Hathi placed Loombar before him on the soft sandy river bank. Magar studied the mechanism of the trap for a minute and, with the concentration of a watchmaker and the dexterity of a surgeon, he set his vice-like jaws to work. It took mere seconds and a loud, collective sigh of relief filled the darkening jungle with joy.

The river began to smile and so did the early evening stars.

The morning dew had not yet been lifted off the grass by the sun god, Surya, when the two hunters returned to a strangely calm jungle. They were eager and excited, sure of finding a great and a varied catch. The tall one picked up a trap. It had a piece of wood sticking out of it, an incomprehensible sight.

'I'll be damned! What do you make of this?' he said in utter disbelief.

'And of this?' said the moustachioed little man.

'I don't believe it. How did they work it out?'

Every trap the men had laid had been made useless, as they soon discovered, going from one to another.

'We've been foxed.'

'Animals! More intelligent than we give them credit for.'

Overhead in a tree, Tota and Lil Squi were watching and listening intently.

'I wish I could say the same about humans,' Lil Squi said and Tota nodded his colourful head.

Jungle Statecraft

Mid-winter was the time of year when a certain type of fish swam upstream in large numbers. They did so to spawn in a great pool where the river cascaded down from the mountains to the plains in a spectacular waterfall. Thus a marvel was created in the lush emerald and sapphire surroundings. When Chanda Mama cast his silvery glance over this awesome sight, it spoke a haunting language that united heaven and earth in ecstatic joy. When dawn swept over it, the spectacle brought the magic of gods to earth. And when Surya lit up the earth, the cascade and the pool stood out as stirring symbols of creation's bewitching jugglery.

No one knew why the fish came to the same pool this time every year, swimming hundreds, perhaps thousands of miles. No one knew. Perhaps even the fish didn't either. All they knew was that they had to come when the earth had gone full circle around the sun, according to their inner clock and calendar. And they came in thousands. One in two did not get back.

For obvious reasons, this was Magar's most favourite time of the year. But catching fish was easier said than done, in spite of the great numbers in which they came. Although the crocodile could move fast, the fish moved faster, much faster.

Fishing, as everybody knows, is a matter of patience. And while Magar was by nature a patient being, he turned into a highly impatient being at this time of the year. Maybe it had something to do with his internal clock, or maybe he simply became too greedy. Whatever it was, his state of mind led to extreme frustration as he chased the abundant but elusive fish.

Magar chased and chased, splashing water with his mighty tail and making a deafening din which resounded all around. Most of the jungle was not bothered by it at all – in fact, it found the sight entertaining. Not so Magar's neighbour and friend, Manu, who lived in a fruit tree directly above the riverbank.

Out of friendship, Manu tried to ignore the noise at first. But having to live with it day after day became a bit too much. Manu complained in a most friendly fashion to begin with. But the usually good-natured and accommodating Magar failed to respond favourably – perhaps he was too preoccupied with catching fish. Manu complained again and again. Magar, driven by frustration, responded in less and less friendly a manner. Manu could not understand his friend's strange new attitude. He complained daily. As a result, Manu's complaints and Magar's responses soon dissolved into an argument.

Unfortunately, the argument got out of hand and strong words were exchanged. Overnight, as it were, the best of friends became the worst of enemies, to every junglebody's utter disbelief.

'I am fed up with the noise you make. Why don't you take your spiky self further upstream and perform your unsocial antics there?'

This was not how one talked to one's friend. Magar didn't like it one bit. He retaliated. It was unlike him, but he couldn't restrain himself. 'Why don't you go and shack up in another tree, preferably well out of our sight? Everybody has had enough of your cheekiness.'

Manu was enraged – no one likes to be told to go and live somewhere else just because it suits somebody else.

'Only someone as thick-skinned as you would make such an impertinent suggestion.'

Already frustrated, Magar lost his cool completely. 'Impertinent?' Magar, doubly furious, splashed his mighty tail furiously, making sure he made a really, really unpleasant noise. 'If I could climb the tree, I would to tell you who's really impertinent. You probably taste the way you sound – nasty.'

'But you can't climb, can you? Nor can you think. Because if you could, you would have apologized and moved upstream or...'

'*Me* apologize to *you*? Me, I only want to swallow you whole.'

Other junglebodies watching and listening were appalled by this ugly altercation – two friends turning on each other like that. This sort of thing was unheard of in their jungle.

'Stop it, you two. This is atrocious. Where are your jungle manners?' Giddar admonished them both severely. But were they listening? They went on saying unsavoury things about each other.

'What does he know of manners? It is his nature to be cheeky and impertinent. It is useless talking to him. God knows how many succulent fishes this useless conversation has cost me. Wish I had never set my eyes on him.'

'What a pity he's unsinkable, Giddar. Wish he wasn't so that he would drown.'

The more insults the two heaped on each other, the more they felt the need to do so. The crocodile gave up the water and came and stationed himself, open-jawed, under the monkey's tree in the hope that the cheekiness personified overhead would break a branch one day and provide him with fast food, a big monkeyburger.

But this was wishful thinking and Manu hopped from branch to branch and tree to tree, sometimes swaying tantalizingly only inches above the creature of the waters, making Magar madder and madder.

The jungle was profoundly alarmed at the escalating verbal hostilities between Manu and Magar, friends of long-standing. Every new day brought a new onslaught of insults, to the jungle's growing concern. How was the jungle to break the deadlock? The junglebodies debated this.

In the days of their friendship, Manu had considered Magar to be an extremely handsome fellow. He used to think that his prehistoric hide was unique and beautiful. No longer. Every morning, Manu woke up in his tree to find Magar – now become a long, hideous beast in his eyes – spread underneath his branch, jaws open, waiting. One morning, Manu plucked the rotten most fruit from the tree, covered it with a ferociously stinging nettle leaf and simply dropped it into the deep and ugly aperture below. As the deadly leaf did its work, the crocodile's grey-brown spiky hide turned purple with anger and he yelled, 'I'll get you yet, cheeky monkey! My day will come yet!'

'Every dog may have his day. But not every crocodile. Certainly not one who has less sense than false hope.'

'Maybe one day lightning will strike the branch you perch on and...'

Lo and behold, one morning, the crocodile's prayers were answered. Dark clouds suddenly gathered over the jungle, sending the birds helter-skelter and the animals to the safety of their respective abodes. Then, accompanied by the fanfaronade of deafening thunder, serpents of lightening stung the blackened sky with their forked tongues and CRASH! a bolt struck that very tree, snapping it in two!

Miraculously, Manu survived. He fell, though, to where the open jaws should have been. But they weren't because, frightened by the heavenly fireworks, Magar had slipped into the safety of the river. Manu had survived twice in two seconds. He made a home in the next tree. As the storm abated, Magar returned.

'It was a near thing. A very near thing. Next time.'

'Haven't you ever heard that lightning never strikes the same place twice?'

'Sometimes it does and it will.'

'You are so ignorant, you make me laugh.'

But this was no laughing matter as far as the jungle was concerned – best friends having become worst enemies. Something had to be done about it and done NOW. A special Panchayat council meeting was held far from the riverbank. Everybody attended, sensing the seriousness of the situation. Even busy Rajah. But as usual, Hathi conducted the proceedings, for when it came to statecraft, the King left matters to the old pillar of wisdom. The same sad question loomed in every junglebody's mind – what were they to do?

'Drown the monkey and hang the crocodile! What a delicious sight – a crocodile hanging from a tree. Ha, ha, ha!' Kurma said, laughing his wobbly head off.

'Do not be frivolous,' Hathi chided him. 'The matter is too serious. We can't have this sort of thing in our jungle.'

'No, we can't,' Loombar said.

It was the way Loombar had said that, with a movement of his head which was neither a nod nor a shake. It gave Hathi a sure feeling that, as usual, Loombar had something up his sleeve. But for once, Hathi was wrong. Not the fox, but the King himself came up with a suggestion.

'I have an idea. It might work, or it might not work. But we must talk about it only in the faintest of whispers. Because trees and bushes have ears. And we do not want anyone outside this august assembly to know, do we? For a leak would only make the whole thing backfire.'

The rest of the discussion took place in whispers so faint, even the writer of this story doesn't know what was discussed. Hathi then brought the meeting to a close by saying, 'Now we all know what we have to do.'

The next day saw Manu frolicking around in another part of the jungle, happily swaying from one tree to another. He was accosted by Lil Squi, Mohan and Mohini.

'I say, what's going on between you and the old croc?' Lil Squi said, jumping to his shoulder.

'The brute hates my guts. Wants to eat me whole.'

'Don't believe a word of it. Only a while ago I sat on his back and had a good chat. It emerged that he is deeply, deeply sorry about things having reached this dreadful impasse between you two.'

'I don't believe you.'

'We were there too, on the riverbank, Mademoiselle and I,' Mohan said. 'And we heard it all. He's aware, what with one thing and another, the argument got out of hand, but is deeply regretful and would like to make amends.'

'Do you expect me to believe that?'

'Believe you me, he wants to apologize because he is really very fond of you,' Lil Squi said, opening her eyes really wide for effect.

'He respects you enormously for your independence and for all the things you've done for others, especially risking your life for Rajah,' Mademoiselle Mohini said.

'Oh, really?'

'Yes, really...,' Lil Squi said, eyes still wide open.

While Manu was engaged in this extraordinary conversation somewhere in the jungle, his arch enemy was at the riverside, being sought out by none other than the King of the Jungle himself. Magar lay semi-immersed in the water, open-mouthed with only his eyes and upper jaw visible, waiting for an unsuspecting foolish fish to oblige. Rajah showed up and leaped into the water for a swim. This was unusual, for the King usually came to the waterfront at dawn or dusk.

'Sire, how nice to see you.'

What Magar really meant was – *this is not your time for a swim, so what are you doing here?*

'Actually, I have come to have a word with you.'

'Oh, really? What about?'

'About this monkey business. I've never seen Manu looking so remorseful.'

This was news to Magar – the last time he saw Manu, he was cheeky, chirpy and happy-clappy as ever.

'In fact, he is deeply depressed and repentant.'

'Oh! What about?'

'About the fact that he finds himself at war with the very junglebody he thinks the world of, due to some silly misunderstanding.'

'I do not understand, Sire.'

'He loves you. He misses your friendship and is desperately sorry that you detest him.'

'I don't detest him. He started it all.'

'He knows and that's why he is so repentant. He wants to say sorry and will do anything to have you back as a friend.'

'I don't believe it, Rajah.'

'Do you doubt your King?'

'Never, Sire.'

'Well, that's all I have to say. Just be nice to him'

'But how can one be nice to someone so rude?'

'Do what your King says. The moment you see Manu again, just say these three little words – I love you – and see the difference it makes. Reflect on it. Good day.' Rajah had a quick dip and was soon gone, leaving Magar totally flummoxed: 'If this is true, why are we behaving like enemies? We must be mad.'

Rajah had gone hardly half a mile when he saw Manu come swinging his way. 'Ah, there you are. I was looking for you all over the place. Do you have a minute?'

'Of course, Majesty.' Manu made a cheeky bow. 'Anything for the King. How may I render myself of service?'

'Just coming from the river.'

'I can see that. You are all wet. Funny time for a swim, though, if I may say so.'

'Saw your friend there.'

'My friend who?'

'Magar, who else? The poor dear is in such a state. He is so utterly sad and so desperately dejected.'

'He seemed nothing of the sort this morning. Only his usual dour self, getting dourer.'

'You know how crocodiles are with their emotions.'

'But why is he so sad and so desperately dejected?'

'Because he thinks that the very junglebody he so adores hates him even more.'

'Who's that, Majesty?'

'You, Manu. *You*. He loves you with all his heart.'

'Me?!' Manu's astonishment was boundless. For the first time in his life, he was lost for words. 'I don't believe a word of it.'

'Do you doubt your King?'

'Of course not, Majesty. But...?'

'Just be nice to him.'

'Majesty, how can one be nice to someone so rude?'

'Do what your King says. The moment you see Magar again, just say these three little words – I love you – and see the difference it makes. Reflect on it. Good day.'

As Rajah disappeared, Manu dangled from the branch of a tree by one hand, reflecting. 'Boy, I'm going to be nice to the old croc because I love him too, my beautiful old friend. Whatever came over us?'

But Manu knew those three little words were the most difficult words to say.

Not far away, there rose a clump of banana trees – a little forest of languid, long, lush leaves with yum yum bunches of Manu's favourite fruit – ripe and yum yum yum. Manu spent an hour there, choosing bananas and thoroughly enjoying himself. It was approaching siesta time. He should be getting back to his tree at the riverside, but he felt a sudden reluctance in his arms and legs to swing homeward. The fact of the matter was he did not want to come face to face with Magar – those three little words were bothering him. He wanted to say them, but he did not know how.

Manu went through the jungle aimlessly, hopping from this tree to that, surprising his junglemates – it was siesta time, he should be back in his tree.

Manu went home only when night fell.

As Surya rose next morning, dispensing welcome warmth on a grateful jungle grown cold during the winter night, Manu rose with him. An equally welcome surprise awaited him in the shape of Magar hurrying up the riverside towards his tree with a warm smile.

'Manu, Manu...'

Those three little words!

'I love you,' Manu and Magar said at the same time.

'What a fool I've been all these days!'

'Fancy a cruise on the river?'

'That'd be cool, Magar, real cool.'

Magar slipped back into the water with Manu on his spiky back and a delighted jungle watched them glide away together.

'Hungry, a bit,' Magar said, 'Early morning, the best time for fishing.'

'I know what. You wait here.'

Magar lay in water facing downstream, his upper jaw raised above the water level at an angle of forty-five degrees. A few yards away, Manu began kicking up the water and sending frightened fishes towards Magar. One handsome specimen, two feet long, went straight into his open jaws as the other junglebodies watched from the riverbank.

'Well, well, well,' Rajah said.

'Now that's what I call friendship, helping one with one's breakfast,' said the silken-tongued fox, Loombar.

'I wish I had friends like that.'

'I bet you do, Rajah,' Kurma said.

The junglebodies saw Manu sit on Magar's back again and watched the two glide away, happy-clappy, happy-clappy. The jungle faces lit up with the sunniest smiles ever – never had jungle life seemed sweeter. Its simple folk had defeated their natural enemies – those abominable men. And now artificial enemies had again become what they really were – natural friends.

Extra Pennies from Heaven

The jungle was used to alarms of all sorts, real and false. No surprise was too shocking, nor any shock too surprising. Danger always lurked around the corner. But the junglebodies took things as they came, and things never came as expected. Yet life in the jungle was ordered. Nobody was unhappy. In fact, the whole jungle brimmed with joy.

The jungle opposed intensely to seeing anyone being wronged, or worse, in pain. And pain, when it came, was not limited to those it affected directly. It touched every jungle heart. For everyone knew it could be them next time around. Early one evening the jungle saw a sight which truly broke its collective heart. It saw a mountain bear with his head covered with a hood and his hands tied up. It was Big Bhaloo, Keeper of the Blue Hills. He was being beaten by sticks and dragged mercilessly through bush and thicket by four men – one of them with a special gun – hell-bent on making a fat profit from this cruel exercise. The jungle sighed in anguish – bushes, trees and all. The junglebodies wanted to do something, but there was that gun to reckon with – it had not just one barrel like the other two hunters', but two!

Overhead, a storm was gathering – low, dark clouds hung ominously above the jungle canopy, bringing night prematurely. With the exception of Manu and Lil Squi, everybody was present at the impromptu riverside meeting, including Rajah – a very rare occurrence indeed.

'We have to do something for Big Bhaloo,' said old Hathi with a heart in flames.

'But what? The men have a double-barrelled gun,' Rajah said.

'If only we could steal it. If only one of us was a robber. Or a thief.'

Rajah knew how exceedingly dangerous a gun with just one barrel could be, but a gun with two? – it would be doubly so! He also knew what old Hathi had said was pure wishful thinking – no junglebody had ever been able to steal a gun from a human.

'Good thought, Hathi. But no one among us was born a thief.'

'No one is born a thief, Majesty,' said Loombar. 'Circumstances make one a thief.'

'Are you suggesting –'

There was a shattering crackle of lightning only yards above the trees under which the assembly was meeting, incandescently lighting up alarmed jungle faces and throwing up a thousand fearful shadows. Deafening thunder followed instantly, drowning Rajah's words. Another infernal storm unleashed itself upon the jungle and, from not far away, they heard the bound and hooded Bhaloo groan pitiably, breaking jungle hearts more and more.

The sudden arrival of the storm caused a change of plans among the men, much to their annoyance. They had hoped to get clear of the jungle before night-fall and sleep in the longed-for comfort of their own beds at home. The ferocity of the storm dictated that they forego that seductive plan and instead rough it out in this abominable jungle.

'What a nuisance!' swore the man with the gun. 'Looks like we have to make camp for the night.'

'Weird jungle, this. Something creepy about it. Creepy and dangerous,' another man said, shivering – he was not only cold, but also afraid.

'And there is a tiger here, lurking in the bushes somewhere,' said man number three.

'He dare not come near us. We have a gun. A double-barrelled gun, firing two shots in one second,' the fourth man boasted.

'I hope for that very reason that he does,' said the gun owner with a smile of anticipation.

'That would be icing on the cake, don't you think? Fetch us twenty grand more, double bag. Extra pennies from heaven.'

Unseen, from a tree nearby, Manu and Lil Squi watched.

'How greedy can they get?' Lil Squi whispered.

'Let's go and alert Rajah,' Manu whispered back.

They raced away and found Rajah conferring with other junglebodies under a rain-soaked tree by the riverside. A serious council meeting seemed to be in progress. Loombar was saying something when Manu and Lil Squi appeared, breathless.

'Majesty, Majesty...'

'What? Pull yourself together, young fellow, and speak coherently,' Rajah said.

'...Phew! Not content with having captured Big Bhaloo, the men hope to bag you as well, Majesty. With your co-operation, that is. Do anything but go near them or announce your presence by issuing unnecessary roars tonight, Majesty. Phew!'

'Ah, talking of thieves, Majesty...,' Loombar said.

'Thieves? Who? Us?' Lil Squi interrupted indignantly. 'Manu and me? Why, you'll never see two more honest junglebodies. What's going on?'

'We are mighty depressed,' Loombar said. 'We are discussing the impossible task of stealing the men's gun and setting poor Bhaloo free. The sight of the two of you lifts our spirits.'

'Does it?' Lil Squi said, her eyes sparkling. 'That's flattering. But how, may I ask?'

'Like this – you two are going to steal the gun...'

'Manu and me steal the gun?' Lil Squi interrupted. 'You are not jesting by any chance?'

'Nope.'

'Loombar dear, it is my duty as a friend to inform you that all is not well with your head. You ought to get it checked.'

'Listen, big little missie. Listen carefully to our plan of action...' The fox unfolded his imaginative, if bizarre, plan. '... The gun stolen, His Majesty and our mighty Hathi will complete the job.'

'What job? And how?' exclaimed Manu and Lil Squi.

'Roaring and trumpeting, they will charge the campsite and put the bad men to flight. Now over to you, Hathi.'

Hathi moved. With amazing ingenuity, he lifted his trunk and gave Lil Squi a little metal object. It was a piece of hooked wire Magar had once extracted from the mouth of a large fish and given to him for safekeeping.

The storm blew itself out in due course. Night spread its raven-black wings, making the jungle look particularly dangerous tonight, as if some invisible force had deliberately made it so. Leaves glinted menacingly in the feeble light of the stars. The usual night noises were heard again, but there was something frightening, even uncanny about them. A rising wind created moving shadows which began to look like ghostly beings. A conspiracy of a supernatural sort seemed to be afoot tonight.

The four men were camped under a tree, huddled around a small fire. The ground was soggy and the light from the fire smoky. The men were warming their hands. Their gun stood by the tree trunk near its owner. Big Bhaloo was tied to another tree nearby. His resounding groans turned the jet black jungle into a ghoulish theatre of sorts. As the night deepened, other sounds from near and far became haunting noises, drenching the jungle in foreboding.

Unseen and unheard, bold Lil Squi, taking her life in the palm of her tiny hand once again, appeared near the gun. She held one end of a piece of string with a fishing hook tied to it. Surreptitiously, she slipped the hook into the trigger-loop of the gun and darted away noiselessly in the darkness.

Lil Squi went and sat next to Manu up in the tree above the hunters' camp. Manu held the other end of the string. His timing was perfect. Quietly and carefully, he pulled the gun upwards and the next moment, the gun was in his hands.

Down below, the men warmed their hands, smoking and making small talk. Then there was a roar of the tiger from not far.

'Here he comes,' whispered the first man.

'On the ready then,' whispered the second.

'I am. But where's my gun? WHERE'S MY GUN?'

'Where's the gun?' said all four of them.

'YOU'VE PUT IT SOMEWHERE! YOU MUST HAVE!,' the first man yelled at the second.

'I haven't! Why should I? And don't shout at me.'

'THEN WHERE HAS IT GONE? WHERE? WHERE? WHERE?!'

'I DON'T KNOW!'

'Stop shouting, you two. We are not deaf. Clearly it has gone,' another of the party said.

The men went looking around the trees and bushes surrounding them. Of course, the gun was not be found anywhere. They came right back to the campfire, deeply troubled and puzzled.

'Guns don't vanish into thin air.' The gun owner was the most troubled of them all. 'This is the work of a demon. Or a ghost.'

'Don't be silly.'

'IT IS THIS FIENDISH JUNGLE! IT IS HAUNTED!...'

At that very instant, the wind lashed out and trees began to wail mournfully and loudly like a multitude of human mourners.

'...HEAR THAT? HEAR THAT?...'

'Don't be silly. You are being superstitious.'

Inexplicably, the night jungle noises amplified tenfold!

'...I AM NOT. AND I AM NOT STAYING HERE A MINUTE LONGER! I AM GETTING OUT! I AM GETTING OUT!'

The jungle symphony became unbearable! The man became hysterical!

'I WANT OUT! OUT! OUT!'

'US TOO,' cried the other two men.

The three frightened men stood up and scampered away as fast as they could. The fourth man had no choice but to join them. Their departure from the scene made the junglebraves' carefully planned attack unnecessary. But Rajah appeared at the campsite with a terrifying roar all the same. So did Hathi, trumpeting. And poor Bhaloo, not knowing what was going on, groaned equally deafeningly. Now the other junglebodies joined them.

With Lil Squi sitting on his shoulder, Manu came down with the gun, two conquering heroes.

'That was a job well done by you honorary thieves,' Rajah said, adding, 'As for me, I feel rather under-employed.'

'Me, too, sire,' Hathi said. Then he turned to Lil Squi. 'Well done, big little missie!'

'But what a cowardly lot! Running away like that before I could make myself useful?' Rajah was disappointed – he had not been able to render himself of service to the jungle family.

'Maybe there'll be another time, sire,'

All of them had for a moment forgotten the reason for all that drama.

'Aren't you forgetting something?' Loombar reminded them.

'Oh, poor old Bhaloo!' Manu yelled and ran and untied him.

'Where am I? What's happened?' Big Bhaloo growled, rubbing his eyes.

'You are in the jungle of joy. And what's happened is you are free. Go back to your loved ones,' said Giddar.

'Do you know your way back?' Manu asked.

'For that I'll rely on my instinct – it never fails.' Big Bahloo ran. But he turned back before disappearing. 'I am grateful. Believe me.'

'We do,' Lil Squi said.

'Thank you.'

'It was nothing.'

'But what are we going to do with this special gun?' Rajah asked. He hated guns, even the ordinary ones.

'What indeed?' Hathi mused. It was an unanswerable question – what could they do with a weapon of their destruction?

'Let's consult our special friend Magar,' Manu suggested. 'He should know. He would do with it whatever he did with the one he once nearly swallowed along with a mutant...'

'Oh, for that, we have to wait till the morning.'

When the morning came, all the junglebodies gathered at the riverside. First they inspected the gun with two barrels, some shaking their heads, others nodding to themselves solemnly. Then they all looked at the great Master of the Waters, requesting with their eyes that the mutants' deadly handicraft be dispensed with as soon as possible.

'A job for you, friend Magar,' Manu broke the silence.

Without a word, the great crocodile took the gun between his immense jaws and dived deep into the river.

The Best Tactic in War

Bibi, the cheetah, was enjoying her siesta with her little one. As the brilliant winter sun rained down, flooding the jungle with glittering gold, mother and cub lay in a tall grass clearing surrounded by dense foliage. A cool, brisk breeze from the blue mountains made the grass, which had the colours of Bibi's lustrous coat, heave like waves of the sea. No other sound could be heard. It was a moment of bliss for the mother – time had come to a standstill and, with her baby at her side, she felt at one with all creation.

A hundred feet away, the barrel of a gun suddenly popped out of the foliage with almost no noise, yet Bibi heard it even though she was asleep. Instinctively knowing it to be man-made, she leapt in the air and turned to grab her cub with her teeth.

BANG!

Bibi disappeared. But the cub was left behind.

The two hunters, scourge of the jungle, rushed out of the foliage, followed by a hired hand who served as their gun-carrier when they were not hunting. The man with the ugly facial scar picked up the cub.

'Pity I missed.' He sounded deeply disappointed.

'But we have the cub. Looks like a kitten. Just like one, a real beauty. Couchicou, couchicou,' said the other hunter, caressing the cub with what seemed genuine fondness. A supreme irony lay in his gesture. 'What a beauty!'

'The mother will go crazy. We ought to let him go, sir,' the hired hand said.

'Left on his own, a hyena will eat him. Or a wolf,' the second man said.

'Anyway, we'll get her later, when she comes looking for him,' said the first.

'But what will we do with him, sir?'

'Sell him to a circus. We'll get a lot of money. Thousands. Cheetahs are rarer than tigers.'

As the evening approached, most of the jungle community turned up at the riverside. The jungle net and jungle telegraph had been busy. Everybody knew what had befallen Bibi and her cub. An air of mourning descended on trees and bushes and the river, too, all of which usually acquired a unique, mysterious beauty at this time of day. But this evening, it was a jungle of sorrow and a river of grieving. This was how the jungle reacted when tragedy struck a member of its community. There was no word in its vocabulary to describe today's tragedy. All the junglebodies stared vacantly at the grey Mother Earth who felt just as they did – forlorn.

'They are taking her cub away. Bibi is going to go mad, poor Bibi. And her poor, poor baby,' Hathi said.

'How can humans do this?' Mohini was tearful – her feminine instincts made her feel acutely the pain of that most unbearable of separations, of a mother and her baby. 'It is unspeakably heartless and cruel.'

'That's humans for you. But do not cry, sweetheart,' Mohan said, edging closer to comfort her.

'Mother and baby. Separated from each other by men lusting for money. It is a crime too terrible for words.' Mohini could not contain her tears. It was woeful.

'It looks so utterly hopeless,' Hathi said, looking at Loombar, hoping he would come up with something again.

But for once, the usually resourceful fox had no idea about what they could do. He sat motionless, devastated like everyone else by what had happened to Bibi and her cub. Nothing in jungle life was more heart-breaking than this, nothing in the whole world. All Loombar could do was stare in front of him at nothing. As Hathi had said, the situation was hopeless.

'Dear God, send us a ray of hope,' Magar said, looking up at the darkening sky, supplicating it for a miracle. The jungle is going to tremble with her roars tonight. It sickens me just to think of her agony.'

No one said anything.

Night fell. Bibi roared crazily in the distance, pathetically looking for her baby. The night groaned with her at her pain. The river flowed on quietly, its every current becoming a lament at Bibi's loss. The jungle community stayed on at the riverside, deriving comfort from being together. Bibi roared and roared.

'It is heart-rending,' Magar said.

'Surely there is something we can do,' Hathi said – this state of helplessness had become unbearable. 'Where is Manu? And Giddar?'

As if the two had been listening to Hathi, there was rustling of leaves above him and in the foliage behind him.

'Manu! Giddar! Where have you two been?'

Manu and Giddar had been on a reconnaissance mission.

'The villains are still in the jungle, camping for the night,' said a breathless Manu.

'Hoping to get Bibi too, obviously,' Giddar added.

'Surely there is something we can do,' Hathi said.

'What can we do against villainous men with lethal fire-arms?' Cheetal said.

Helpless as they were, the junglebodies would not give up hope. They stayed on and saw the night advance and the sky gradually fill up with stars, thousands of pinpricks of light peeping from that vast, deep, steel-blue expanse. The stars had no beauty about them tonight, only a deep sadness. The cool light they shed came bathed in invisible tears.

Half a mile away, the poachers were sitting around a lively campfire which crackled every few seconds, illuminating their greedy faces. Between them was a small, crudely-crafted wooden cage in which the cub whimpered helplessly. All around them was pitch black, the cold air thick with intimation once again of something awful about to happen. Somewhere in the distance, Bibi roared pitifully. It was a special roar, a howl – that of a demented mother who had her baby snatched from her. It was the howl of immeasurable pain. It made the cub cry so, it could have melted even a heart of stone. But the hearts of these men were made of a substance harder than stone – greed.

'Mark my words, she'll be here soon. Be on the ready,' said the moustachioed hunter, taking his gun in his hands.

'I am,' said the other. 'Let her come. I promise not to miss this time.'

'We'll have her dead and the cub alive.'

'More than we'd had hoped for.'

Back at the riverfront, the junglebodies still sat staring at nothing, thinking. Somewhere deep in the jungle, Bibi roared dementedly.

'Bibi's going mad. Surely there is something we can do?' Old Hathi was not prepared to give up.

'Counsel her at least,' Giddar said.

'She won't listen to anyone in the state of mind she's in.'

'She would maul us to death if we went anywhere near her,' Cheetal said.

'My biggest fear is that she will go to the poachers' camp to retrieve her baby and get shot,' Hathi said. His remark had a shattering finality.

'Not if we take steps to avoid that happening.' Loombar spoke at last.

'What steps, Loombar?' everybody said, their mood suddenly becoming a little hopeful – they knew foxy old Loombar.

'Let's do to these mutants what we were not able to do to the last lot.'

'What, charge them? How can we without Rajah?' Hathi said.

'We can. Or rather, you will, Hathi. It's going to be risky, even dangerous. But may prove fruitful.'

'Nothing ventured, nothing gained,' Manu mused.

'We are all going to play a part in it. Wish Rajah was with us tonight. As he is not, you, Hathi, would be playing the leading role. The most dangerous, too. So take charge.'

'Of what, Loombar? And how?'

'Thunder into the men's camp crashing through the trees, making the mother of all earthly noises. Take the wicked men unawares.'

'They'll shoot me.'

'They won't if you take them by surprise – they are not expecting you. Only Bibi.'

'Correct,' Manu said, clicking his fingers. 'They say surprise is the best tactic in war.'

'Cause sudden and total pandemonium.'

'What happens next?' Manu asked.

'This is where you come in, Manu, to do your bit. Do you understand?'

'I think I do. But I also think it is rather risky, very risky. Don't you?'

'Nothing ventured, nothing gained!' Kurma said.

'We've all got to be there at the same time, all of us. And we've all got to make as much noise as possible, synchronized to perfection. Scream, yell, howl. Loudly. Take them by storm. Let them think hell has let itself loose.'

'I'll take an odd bullet if it comes to that. I have a thick enough skin. Must put it to good use for the jungle family's sake,' Hathi smiled, adding, 'Wish Rajah was with us, though. I really do. He would have full employment tonight.'

At the poachers' camp, the three men sat around the fire, talking in whispers. Guns in their laps, they warmed their hands, alert and anxious. The caged cub whimpered miserably like a lost kitten near them. From not too far away now, Bibi roared angrily. She was wailing for her lost baby.

'She is coming. How far do you think she is?' said the one with arched eyebrows.

'A few hundred yards?' replied the other.

'With her dead and the cub alive, why that would be icing on the cake! Fetch us thousands more. Now if that is not luck, what is?' The man with the arched

eyebrows smiled the smile of someone who sees a lot of money unexpectedly coming his way.

Suddenly, all hell broke loose. They heard an almighty noise and saw a jumbo elephant trumpet deafeningly and crash through the foliage to their camp site, bringing trees down in his path. At the same time, the jungle erupted with yet more noise as all junglebodies spread around the hunters' camp filling the night with resounding cries, yells and howls. The three men knew not what had hit them. So shockingly total was the surprise, they did not have the time or the sense to pick up their guns. In utter panic, they ran helter-skelter into the surrounding darkness to save themselves from being trampled over by what seemed to be a rogue elephant.

Manu leapt into action. Jumping from a tree, he ran past the campfire, grabbed the cage and disappeared in the darkness. It all took a mere ten or twelve seconds. Soon it was all quiet again in the jungle night – just the hoot of an owl and a family of hyenas laughing somewhere in the distance. Hathi picked up a gun with his trunk and smashed it over and over again against a tree till its barrel twisted and the butt broke. He dealt with the second gun the same way.

Presently at the riverside, the junglebodies met again. In their midst sat the little wooden cage.

'Open it, young sir,' Loombar said to Manu. 'Only you have hands. We have paws.'

Manu opened the cage and caressed the cub.

'So beautiful and free at last. To think the men wanted to put him in a circus cage for money!' Hathi said.

There was a roar. It was very near.

'Here she is. Let's leave the cub here and withdraw.'

The cub began to play with Hedgy the hedgehog, like a child playing with a toy. The foliage parted and Bibi appeared, growling softly with unconcealed joy. She licked her cub and growled again with immense relief and measureless motherly love. Then with her teeth she picked him up by the scruff of his neck and vanished into the jungle.

'What a wonderful sight!' Loombar said.

The night had suddenly become wonderful, supremely wonderful.

'It was worth it, the risk and all. And look. Not a scratch,' Hathi said.

'As they say, all's well that...,' Magar bellowed, slipping into the water. They saw him glide away in Chanda Mama's pale light, a luminescent line leaving an ever-expanding triangle behind it. Then Magar ducked underwater, and nothing was left of that line, only a wondrous mercury-shimmer which stretched to the left and right as far as the eye could see.

'But where have Manu and Giddar disappeared to again?' Loombar asked, looking around for them.

'You should know,' Hathi replied.

Manu and Giddar had slipped away to follow the hunters and find out what they were up to now. Beaten, bent and broken, the men were making their way ignominious retreat out of the jungle when Manu and Giddar caught up with them. They heard the one with the arched eyebrows say: 'I have had enough of this blasted jungle. I'm never going to set foot here again.'

'Nor me,' said the one with the silly moustache.

'Good idea and GOOD RIDDANCE!' Manu and Giddar jubilated, turning their backs on them.

A Jungle Celebration

The bad men had been comprehensively defeated. The villainous schemers had been humiliated by simple junglebodies who had neither their ruthless cunning nor their superior means. The men would never come back. The jungle had seen the last of them.

And good riddance, as Manu and Giddar had said!

The relief felt by the junglebodies was immense, as was their joy. The occasion needed to be marked with a suitable celebration. The eager junglebodies, never ones to postpone an opportunity to have fun, appointed the very next evening for it. So, as the first stars appeared and a light evening breeze rustled through the trees, the bushes at the riverside parted and, in ones and twos they all turned up with fresh and glad-to-be-here faces – with the exception of Rajah who was, as usual, elsewhere.

The Lord of the Underworld, Ananta, happened to pass by while on his way to meet his paramour, Anantin. The jungle froze when it saw that long sinuous black line glistening in the starry light. But Ananta had the friendliest of intentions. He did something he rarely did. He joined in, though just for a minute or two. And he was warmly welcomed by all.

A variety show was their unanimous choice, and everybody took part. The show's main themes would be: make a speech on a topic of the gathering's choice, impersonate anybody of one's own choosing or give a performance of just any sort.

But who would volunteer to be the first on the stage?

Be the first on the stage? No one wanted to be the first on the stage. Enthusiasm began to dwindle. They all looked away, hoping someone else would take up the challenge.

This, clearly, was not a good start. Someone had to set an example. Someone decisive. But, again, who?

Looking to his right and left, Manu stepped forward. He cleared his throat loudly and said with a certain swagger, 'Me. I'll go first.'

'Bravo! Bravo!'

'But what will you do, Manu?' Mohan asked.

'I will orate.'

'Orate? What's that?' Lil Squi asked Mohan at whose feet she sat, a nut of some sort between her tiny claws.

'Make a speech, you know. To impress.'

'Oh, that? I know. Okay, Manu. You are on.'

Manu wanted to be given a few minutes.

'So that I may compose myself. All great actors need to do that, you know,' he said and disappeared into the bushes. There, he rehearsed his piece, addressing the trees as 'Ladies and Gentlemen...' Five minutes later, he returned to a noisy reception. He took a deep breath and roared loudly a few times, opening his mouth wide.

'A kingdom works only if everybody knows his or her place and station in it. You all know your place and station in this kingdom. All you have to do is just stick to it. Do not pretend to be anyone or anything other than who or what you are. And you all know who and what you are. Now guess who and what I am. Thank you for your attention.' Manu roared again a couple of times before leaping on to a low-lying branch of his tree.

Nobody was impressed.

'That's not oration. It's impersonation,' Khargosh said.

'Impostortion, I would say,' Kurma declared.

'Boo! Who's next?' Mohan asked.

'You, pretty boy,' Manu snapped.

'Yes, you,' chorused all present.

'Me? why me?'

'Because you were rude to gallant Manu, you booed,' Hathi said.

'Sorry, Manu, my friend. I apologize. But I am not a public speaker.'

'Then do something else. Just dance. You are good at that,' Loombar said.

'For that, I need to be in the mood. For that I need Mademoiselle Mohini before me. Or I cannot dance,' Mohan said, bowing towards Mohini.

'Step forward, Mademoiselle.' Loombar, too, bowed towards her – Loombar could be the most courteous of creatures when the occasion demanded.

Blushing, Mohini stepped forward. The mood took Mohan. He fanned out his magnificent tail and danced his steps of enchantment – the lustrous blue-green-turquoise-lapis lazuli magic enthralling them all. This was jungle chic at its best. There was thunderous applause and Mohini blushed and blushed.

'I say, Mohan,' Chuhi said. 'Quite a ladies' man you are!'

The next to come was Giddar. He was given a subject to speak on – jungle manners.

'The jungle gives us food. It gives us shelter. The jungle is our home. It's a beautiful home, rich and lush and abundant. We love our home. Contrary to the popular belief, might is not right in the jungle. In the jungle, you live and let live. You do not interfere. You let others do what they want to do. That is good jungle manners.'

This went down well.

'Well said, Giddar. Well said,' said Loombar, realizing at once that he should not have spoken at all. For it drew attention to himself with regard to the question – who next?

'Loombar!'

'I was dreading this. Like the Beautifullestest One, I am not a public speaker either. And unlike him, I can't dance. Nor am I in a position to even if I could. Ask someone else.'

'We want Loombar! We want Loombar!'

'Oh, dear,' Kurma said. 'Looks like you have to make a speech. So stand and deliver, dear boy.'

Nobody told Loombar what to speak about. As there was only one subject he knew, he decided to make his speech quickly and have done with it before the others had the time to think of an awkward topic. Looking suitably suave and smooth, the silken-tongued Loombar stood up and looked his audience in the eye.

‘Friends, junglebodies and junglemates. I am painfully aware of the reputation men have given me. I am called crafty, full of guile, wily. I know self-praise is no recommendation, but nothing is farther from the truth. All my actions are borne out of one simple need common to us all – self-preservation. Like my worthy friend Khargosh, I run when chased by men. What men don’t like about me is the fact that they cannot catch me. I outwit them. Now is it a crime to outwit those who are out to annihilate you?’

‘No, it’s not,’ Ananta said, smiling broadly. ‘But you have outwitted us, too. You didn’t give us time to choose a topic for you to speak on, crafty old Loombar, you.’

There was good-hearted laughter all around – this was good going. But who was next.

‘Ananta, Ananta!’

The great cobra looked from left to right, uneasily. He had never ever been the centre of attention, simply because he was seldom seen, but whenever he was, everybody left him alone. They did so not only out of fear, but essentially because that was the law of the jungle – you left each other alone, as Giddar had just said.

‘I’m sorry, I haven’t got the time. I’m on my way to meet Lady Anantin. And I’m already late. I must be off.’

‘Ananta! Ananta!’

The resounding chant of his name revealed how popular he really was, feared yet popular, however paradoxical that might seem. The junglebodies were not going to miss this rare opportunity. They suggested a quick guest appearance.

‘Ananta! Ananta! Ananta!’

Ananta realized he had to give in and do something. He wished, though, that Anantin was around to inspire him as Mohini had inspired Mohan. That not being the case, he thought of her and did the only thing he knew – he danced. He fixed the evening with his hypnotic eyes and moved in sinuous curves, swaying his hooded head with its godly mark to the rhythm of imagined godly music. His dance was haunting. It was intoxicating – the snake had charmed the jungle, the stars...the evening itself!

‘Wow!’ Chuhi said. ‘What a charmer you are, Ananta!’

'And now you must excuse me. Mustn't keep Lady Anantin waiting,' Ananta said and gracefully glided out of sight.

Hathi came next. He was given a really, really difficult subject to speak on – the sky.

'Oh, no!' Hathi moaned.

'Oh, yes!'

'The sky? No one can speak about the sky without speaking about the stars in the sky.'

'If anyone can, you can. So put your thinking cap on and rise to the occasion.

Hathi had no choice.

'But stars are only grains of glowing sand flung apart, suns and moons and galaxies all, pinpoints of light emitted or reflected.'

'Hear, hear! But what is the sky?'

'The sky is an extension of the space between you and me. And it is limitless. It continues forever.'

'May I dare ask a question?' Manu raised a hand. 'How can anything be limitless? The sky is not a thing. It's nothing. It's empty space.'

'But the space between you and me is not empty. It is full of the air we breathe,' Cheetal said.

'Too true, too true. But the air only exists in the earth's atmosphere for a mere few miles. Then there's nothing. And far, far away in the sky are countless galaxies and beyond them, nothing, beneath them, nothing, above them, nothing. Only empty space.'

'I do not understand. But it is fascinating. So go on, go on!' Magar said.

'Yes, go on, Hathi. It's also stimulating,' Chuhi said.

'The stars and galaxies were made somehow. But space was not made, because it is nothing.'

'How can it be nothing and yet be there? I do not understand, my dear Hathi.' Magar looked pained.

'Nobody does, my dear Magar.'

'Do humans understand? Can they explain ... ?'

Nobody wanted to hear about humans. Not tonight.

'Ugh!' they groaned, as if there was a bad odour.

'Please, Magar.' Manu pinched his nose with two fingers.

'Sorry, I shouldn't be mentioning humans – we are having such a wonderful time. Who's performing next? You, Khargosh.'

'Oh, dear. I'm hopeless at this sort of thing. Honestly.'

'You can at least try,' Lil Squi said.

'Can I count on some support, and give a joint performance – with, say, Loombar, Giddar and Manu maybe?'

'Sure,' Lil Squi said, somersaulting in the scented evening air for no reason – a delicious performance in itself.

'If the other three agree,' Hathi said.

'We do,' said Loombar, Giddar and Manu.

'Need a bit of makeup and some props. Give us a minute or two, will you?'

The foursome disappeared into the foliage. When they reappeared, the hare was dressed up as a High Court Judge, the fox and the jackal as hunters with chains around their necks, and the monkey as a policeman. The policeman carried a grand-looking chair in one hand and pulled the hunters by their chains. He put the chair down for the Judge.

A trial was about to take place.

'All stand for the Judge,' the policeman said, solemnly.

The spectators stood up as the Judge took his seat. The policeman brought the culprits before him.

Judge: The Following Are The Charges Against You. One, You Intimidate All Junglebodies. Do You Plead Guilty Or Not Guilty?

Hunters: Not Guilty, Your Honour.

Judge: Two, You Shoot Junglebodies. Do You Plead Guilty Or Not Guilty?

Hunters: Not Guilty, Your Honour.

Judge: Three, You Nearly Shot Manu. What Do Have To Say In Your Defence?

Hunters: He Foiled Our Plans, Your Honour.

Judge: Four, You Laid Traps To Capture Junglebodies.

Hunters: We Are Hunters, Your Honour. It's Our Profession.

Judge: Five, You Took Shots At The Tiger.

Hunters: We Are Hunters, Your Honour.

Judge: You Did So For His Magnificent Skin Which Would Have Sold For A Lot Of Money.

Hunters: It Is Our Profession, Your Honour.

Judge: (Addressing all present) Members Of The Jury, Do You Find The Defendants Guilty Or Not Guilty On All Five Counts?

All Present: Guilty! Guilty!

Hunters: (Protesting loudly) We Are Not, Your Honour. We Are Not.

Judge: You Are Heartless And Cruel Mercenaries. As Judge Of This Court, It Is My Duty To Sentence You. I Sentence You To Be Hanged By The Neck Till ...

Hunter 1: (Pleading) Your Honour!

Hunter 2: Your Honour!

All Others: (Jubilantly) Hooray!

Just then, there was a roar from behind the trees, making everybody tremble – the Judge, the Jury and the convicts. And Rajah appeared – eyes glaring, setting the riverside alight with fear, the stars descending to earth to do obeisance and the evening bowing to him in admiration. Rajah looked magnificent, every inch a king – beautiful and mighty. He also looked perplexed – whatever in heaven's name was going on in his jungle? Then the penny dropped.

'Showtime in the jungle? Well, well, well! Am I too late to take part?'

'No, Majesty. Just in time to give us a glimpse of your limitless talents,' Manu said.

'Well, well, well! Why not? What should I do now? I know what. I shall impersonate. But who? Oh, I know.'

Rajah laughed and looked around. His eyes fell on Lil Squi. He laughed again and rolled on the ground like her, arching his tail like her, and jumped up and down like her. Finally, he spoke like her – sweetly:

'Lil Squi is my name

I have no claim to fame

But to entertain you is my game

My teeth are sharp and my tail is long

And one last thing – I am not tame.'

The performance was so convincing, it made everybody laugh and clap furiously, even Lil Squi, who shed a tear of joy. Then she ran and went and sat on Rajah's back.

'Now you are,' Lil Squi piped.

The applause was thunderous. The like of it had never been heard in the jungle. Rajah made a bow. Then another and another and another.

Your Honour,' he addressed the Judge still sitting in his chair. 'Your Honour, pity the accused are not real men. Had they been, I would have saved you the trouble of having to find the rope to hang them.'

The White Cross of Destruction

In the dead of night, six men came to the jungle with two loaded mules. Their leader selected a tree, painted a white cross on its trunk with a brush and ordered his men to dig under it. The men dug a deep trench and placed what the mules had carried at the bottom. Then they filled it up with dug-out earth, levelling it with the ground, and went away with their mules, puzzling the jungle immensely.

When morning rose, many junglebodies gathered under that tree to inspect the ground. They raised their eyebrows and shook their heads as they tried to divine what the men had buried there at such an ungodly hour?

'Treasure,' Giddar said, convinced.

'What is treasure?' Khargosh asked.

'You know – gold, diamonds, jewels.'

'I've never seen treasure. I would love to have some,' Khargosh said.

'Me too,' Mohan said.

'What will you do with it? One has to know what to do with treasure, otherwise it is useless. And you don't, Khargosh.'

'If I had some diamonds and jewels, I would give them to Mademoiselle,' Mohan said.

'Ahhh...!' said all present, looking at Mohini as she looked away bashfully, stamping her left foot in sweet confusion.

'But it is not treasure that's buried here,' Loombar said. 'It's other things I saw, long things wrapped carefully in some strange material with a sheen.'

'We'd never know, would we? Unless one of us was able to excavate,' Hathi said.

'I can. Shall I have a go?' Khargosh said.

'Take you ages to dig that deep,' Hathi said.

'I don't mind.'

'Go ahead then, if you have the will and the stamina,' Loombar said.

'I have plenty of both. Plenty. Do you want to lend a paw, Loombar?'

'No thank you. I have a catalogue of other things to attend to.'

Full of enthusiasm, Khargosh started to excavate. He dug and dug, shedding drops of perspiration. For the first hour, the others hung around and watched. It didn't make for fascinating watching. They got bored and, one by one, they went away. But the determined Khargosh continued to dig deeper and deeper. Hours later, he emerged with a round metallic object the size of an average mango, only a little rounder in shape and heavier, with a pin sticking out at the top. Khargosh was deeply disappointed.

'This is no treasure. It neither glitters like gold nor does it shine like a jewel. And I am missing lunch for it? What a fool I've been.' The exercise had made him ravenous.

Dropping the object on the ground, Khargosh sprinted away to find some food to fill his desperately empty belly. As he left, Manu appeared on the scene. Being incurably curious, he picked up the metal thing. Lil Squi came running after him.

'I've got a jewel. I've got a jewel,' Manu sang.

'Let me see. Let me see.'

'I've got a jewel. I've got a jewel,' singing, Manu ran and climbed up a very tall tree, hotly chased by the curious Lil Squi.

'Be a sport. Let me see.'

Manu climbed to the very top of the tree and settled down to examine the jewel. He pulled out the pin and there was an urgent hissing sound. Frightened, Manu flung the jewel away. As the jewel hit the ground sixty feet below, there was an earth-shattering explosion and hundreds of Panchchi Loag shot out of all the trees in the jungle cawing, crowing and crying.

'My O my! What was that?!' Manu was dumbfounded.

'An explosion, by the sound of it,' Lil Squi said.

They hurried down to see. A pallid cloud of pungent smoke shrouded the area of the explosion. Very soon other junglebodies turned up to investigate the cause of that dreadful noise.

'It was louder than any gun I ever heard,' Manu told them.

'I bet that metal mango had thunder trapped in it.'

'What metal mango, Manu?' asked Loombar.

'Oh, dear. Was it the thing I'd dug out of the trench?' Khargosh asked.

'Describe it to us,' Hathi said.

'It was the size of an average mango, but much heavier with lines etched on it.My friend here says thunder was trapped in it.'

'It was no thunder,' Hathi said. 'There is a strong smell in the air. It is the same sort as you get when men fire a gun. Only much stronger.'

'Are you saying it was a big bullet disguised as a metal mango?' Manu said.

'Something like that,' Hathi replied.

'Good thing I had the sense to throw it away. Otherwise I would have become mango chutney. My O my! My luck was running good.'

'Shall I extract another one from down there, Hathi?' Khargosh said, half trembling – he didn't really want to touch another of those.

'You'd better not – we don't want carnage here. It was extremely fortunate that Manu and big little missie were up in the tree when it went off.'

'What do we do then?' Loombr asked.

'Watch developments as they develop,' Hathi answered.

'Everybody, keep your ears to the ground. And you, winged angels, keep your eyes open.'

'We always do when we are flying,' the Panchchi Loag replied.

'Report the moment you see something suspicious.'

'We will.'

Early one morning, four swarthy-looking young men entered the jungle. They had two spades between them. They were not the hunting type, because they had a lost look on their faces – they were new to the jungle. They went looking from tree to tree till they saw the one with the white cross. Then the men started digging and all the jungle watched them from a hundred secret spots. The men unearthed

plastic explosives and timers and metal mangoes which had thunder trapped in them. First the men hid them under their clothing, then they hid the spades in bushes near the marked tree. That done, the men made their way out of the jungle.

'My O my!' Manu cried, opening his eyes wide.

'Ominous, this. Very ominous,' said the Panchchi Loag.

'I wonder what they are going to do?' worried Loombar asked.

'I dread to think what. Angels, follow them and watch their every move. They are up to no good,' Hathi said.

The men hurried out of the jungle and made their way to town as the birds shadowed their movements. Two of the men went to the railway bridge and stuck things under it. The other two stole their way to the municipality building and shoved similar things in a dustbin. At both places, the two men shook hands and parted company, each going off alone in a different direction. Some time later the city shook, even more violently than the jungle had done the other day.

BANG! BANG!

Petrified, the Panchchi Loag flew back fast to report: 'Those men were terrorists.'

'Terrorists? Who are terrorists, Hathi?' Manu asked.

'Mass killers.'

'OF HUMANS?!' cried all present in one voice.

The junglebodies were astounded. The first and foremost law of the jungle was that no junglebody ever killed without hunger. They simply could not understand why men with all their superior knowledge killed other men.

'BUT WHY?'

'Because they are misguided and brainwashed. So they kill and hurt innocent people to cause anarchy and gain control.'

'That's not on,' Khargosh said.

'DEFINITELY NOT!'

'Where do we go from here, O Wise One?' Loombar said. These men will come back to their hidden arsenal and take more stuff and maybe kill hundreds of innocent men, women and children. I knew they were up to no good.'

'What we do is the following. Look, that first lot of men must have been rather dumb, for they have left their paint and paint brush.' The elephant took the brush in his trunk and painted a cross on every tree in sight. 'Now we'll see what they get up to.'

The same four men came back early another morning – and got a shock, the strength of a bolt of lightning – a white cross was painted on the trunk of every tree around.

'Sabotage! Sabotage!' hissed one man through his teeth, his eyes full of hatred.

'Which is our tree? We could spend months digging and never find our weapons. Someone has made a monkey of us,' spat another with venom in his voice.

'We will come back with the Boss. He'll recognize the right tree.'

The men hurried out of the jungle to get to their leader.

'We've got to do something before they come back,' Hathi said, urgently.

'What, for instance?' Manu asked.

'There's something you can do, Manu. You. Only you.'

'What?'

'Khargosh, be a good fellow and dig out another metal mango. On the double. Time's in short supply,' Hathi said.

Khargosh dug up another metal mango. Everybody craned to inspect it.

'It appears to go off only when you pull out this wretched pin,' Manu pointed out.

'Well, then the obvious thing to do is not to pull it out,' Kurma said.

'Hardly the time for your wisecracks, Mr Wobble,' Loombar said, quite annoyed at the tortoise's insensitivity.

'Only a light-hearted quip, Loombar. Don't be so touchy.'

Hathi ignored this untimely interjection. He took matters in his hand.

'Manu, now listen carefully. You've got to go to town double-quick time with this metal mango thing. Turn up at the police station and let the policemen see you with it. Thereafter, it is up to you to make them come here. Use your ingenuity, imagination and initiative. Wrap it up in leaves so that no one else recognizes it. Go!'

'Resist the temptation of pulling out the pin,' Kurma whispered.

'And come back in one piece,' Mohini said, planting a peck on his cheek.

'Good luck, dear Manu.'

'Thank you, Mohini. But how will I find the police station?'

'We'll lead you to it,' said the Panchchi Loag from the trees.

Just as Manu was about to set off, Lil Squi called out: 'Wait. I'll go with you. To give you strength. One and one make eleven. True. Ask Chuhi.'

The police station in town turned out to be a large intimidating building painted yellow. It had a high wall all around, making it look like a fort. The metal mango covered in leaves in one hand, the other on his hip and Lil Squi by his side, Manu did not know what to do next. The Panchchi Loag settled on the branches of the trees inside the walls.

'Use your ingenuity...' Hathi's words rang out in his ears. Manu scaled the wall and Lil Squi followed, trembling – the fear of the unknown and unfamiliar world of humans beginning to overwhelm her. But bravely, she remained by Manu's side.

A police inspector was sitting on a chair in the garden, eating fruit. Two policemen were in attendance. Manu threw away the leaves covering the metal object and held it up.

'Run for cover,' a policeman shouted. 'The monkey's got a hand grenade.'

'Shall I shoot him down, sir?' said the second policeman.

'No,' the Inspector said. 'There's more to this than meets the eye. What do monkeys like?'

'Fruit, sir. Bananas.'

The Inspector threw a banana to the monkey: 'Come here, little fellow. Tell us where you got it from. If only monkeys could talk.'

Manu helped himself to the banana, but kept his distance.

'Tell us where you got it from. Are there any more there?'

The monkey climbed back on the wall and started jumping up and down, making funny faces and funny noises. The squirrel sat at his feet.

'Sir, I'd better shoot him before he throws it at us.'

'I think he is trying to say something. He wants us to follow him. Isn't that so, little fellow?'

Manu jumped up and down, scratching himself.

'That's right, isn't it? You want us to follow you.'

The monkey and the squirrel then jumped to the other side of the wall, a clear sign. The three men climbed after them and followed them. They followed them all the way to the ammunition dump in the jungle.

'Incredible!' cried the Inspector. 'The terrorists' ammunition dump. We can catch them now.' The Inspector then ordered one of his men, 'Run and get reinforcements. We'll lay an ambush and arrest them.'

In due course, several armed policemen arrived. They hid around the buried arsenal. They didn't have to wait very long. The terrorists came, all ten of them, and looked from one tree with its white-painted cross to the next, mystified.

'The game's up! SURRENDER!' the Inspector shouted through a hailer, frightening the hidden junglebodies with the volume of his voice.

A terrible shoot-out followed. All the jungle trembled. Two terrorists were shot. The others surrendered. Two pickup trucks tore their way through the jungle with more policemen. They pushed the handcuffed bad men into one. Then they dug up the ditch and recovered the infernal arsenal – rifles, machine guns, grenades etc. That accomplished, they went away, leaving the jungle in what it valued most of all – peace. But they left something behind – a heap of bananas and a big bag of nuts.

The jungle watched, its eyes laden with equal measures of puzzlement and curiosity.

'Manu,' said Loombar. 'If you were a man, they would have given you a medal.'

'Prefer bananas, actually. Try one, Loombar. Awfully good.'

'You know I hate bananas.'

'You try one, Hathi dearest.'

'Thank you. I adore bananas.'

'Have lots, then. Help yourself.'

'Good work, that was, I must say,' Hathi said, helping himself. 'Good work.'

'Even cheeky old me can be useful at times.'

'We have a hero in our midst.'

'And an artist, too.'

A Jungle Wedding

The junglebodies called it the Singing Hill. In fact, it was a mound of porous, granular earth twice the height of Manu when he stood upright. A humming sound could sometimes be heard coming out of it, lending it an aura of a living being. How else could a pile of earth issue forth notes that came only when the chords of a musical instrument were plucked? It was a living mystery among the junglebodies. But then the jungle held many mysteries. So all junglebodies accepted the presence of this mound amongst them as they did that of each other, never doubting it felt about them the same way.

The Singing Hill had been there for as long as anyone could remember, even the oldest of them all, Hathi. From time to time, it hummed a lullaby – to itself? Or to Surya when it chose to shine with an extra mellow sparkle? Or to the invisible breezes when they withheld their breath from the jungle? Maybe it addressed its song to Chanda Mama when the distance between night and day was at its longest.

Sometimes, Ananta came in swiftly moving curves of electrifying grace and raised himself high and spread his glorious hood and bore his eyes into the humming mound and swayed from side to side. Then, the Panchchi Loag came and settled in the surrounding trees to watch this most magical of jungle sights – its deadliest being transported under the spell of the song of the Singing Hill!

Sometimes, Mohan and his Mademoiselle came too. And if and when the mood took him, Mohan danced his steps of enthrallment. His dance not only filled Mohini's heart to the brim with joy, but, Mohan was sure, affected that of the Singing Hill in the same way. For he knew it had a heart, otherwise how could it sing – you can sing and dance only if you have a heart. Then for days and weeks they forgot it existed.

Manu's new daily routine of a morning river cruise with Magar – they were greater friends than ever now – lasted well into one afternoon, an indescribable sun-soaked heaven of honey and gold. It was time for a banana or two or three or more and then...and then, of course, his daily forty winks. After his feast, as Manu perched in his new tree on the riverbank, reviewing the jungle goings-on in his head and fast approaching the point when sleep, sweet sleep, would swamp it, something on the ground inland caught his eye – a long black line. And it was moving! A moving line!

Ever curious, Manu descended from the tree to take a closer look. He had a shock. Thousands upon thousands of big black ants, *kidis*, were hurrying away top speed, as if they were being chased by some loathsome enemy. They fled one after the other, single file. Manu ran to see where they were going, but he couldn't reach the head of the line. So he ran back to see where they were coming from. Manu ran and ran and had another shock – the ants were coming from cracks at the base of the Singing Hill! This was baffling, most baffling. With bated breath, Manu asked a fine specimen, a mother of ten: 'Kidi, dear sister Kidi, where are you racing to in such feverish haste? Please tell me, for it fills me with profound concern for you all.'

'To save ourselves,' the black moving dot replied, baffling Manu even more.

'From what?'

'From being destroyed in our own home.'

'Oh, please, Kidi, explain what you mean?'

'I've no time. I've told you all I know,' the racing Kidi said and raced on along the moving black line which disappeared under bushes before reappearing again just past them.

Bewildered as he had never been, Manu ran yet again, this time to find some kindred junglespirit to discuss this bizarre matter with. And guess who he ran into? – old Hathi, looking his usual relaxed self. Hathi was out to seek the river for a good lie down in the mud and a refreshing bath.

'Come see an extraordinary sight. You won't believe your own eyes.'

'Oh, yes?'

When Hathi saw the endless procession of ants coming from the Singing Hill, he stood well back. He gasped and his eyes popped. This alarmed Manu. He began to scratch his chest.

'This means one and only one thing,' Hathi sighed. 'An earthquake.'

'What's an earthquake? What does it mean?'

'It means destruction of us all. But I do not have the time to explain. Run and call everybody. Run, run, run! Tell them to tell others to meet us in a clearing well away from the trees and the river. The grassy glade down south. As soon as possible. Then I'll explain.'

'What about Magar?' Manu was worried about his friend.

'Don't worry about Magar. The Lord of the Waters will be all right in the earthquake. Now run.'

The monkey ran this side, the elephant the other, both shouting hysterically: 'AN EARTHQUAKE IS COMING, BRINGING DESTRUCTION TO US ALL! GATHER IN THE GRASSY GLADE DOWN SOUTH STRAIGHT AWAY!'

Within minutes, all the jungle had gathered at the grassy glade, demanding an explanation for the furore.

'But who is an earthquake? How is he going to destroy us all? How can any one? Will you kindly enlighten us? You've ruined my siesta, do you know?' Rajah was clearly not amused.

'Mine, too.' Nor was Khargosh.

'He will come any minute after the last of the ants has vacated the Singing Hill,' Hathi said in a voice so serious, it filled all assembled with foreboding. What on earth was he talking about?

Except for Hathi, no one knew what an earthquake was. The elephant's demeanour and tone left no doubt in every junglebody's mind that it was something awesome. Curiosity instantly turned to despair and despair to gloom. Many questions were haphazardly hurled at Hathi, whose head was already full of worries of the jungle.

'Who is an earthquake?'

'Is he a mutant with a super gun?'

'How will he come?'

'From which direction?'

'What does he look like, a demon?'

Hathi did his best to explain.

'The earth will rumble. She will tremble and then she will tilt. Like this.'

Lifting his left front foot, Hathi swayed from left to right.

'But how can she?' Loombar asked. 'The earth is firmly embedded in herself.'

'The earth will quake, and that's why what she does is called an earthquake, as if a giant sitting inside her belly has given her a mighty kick.'

'How do you know?' Rajah said.

'Because the ants have abandoned their ancestral home. Whenever they do that, it heralds an earthquake. They live close to the earth's interior, so they know. Some mysterious signal from her informs them.'

'So what's going to happen?'

'Great trees will fall to the ground like colossuses who have lost their balance. The earth will open up in great cracks. The river will tilt, inundating the jungle.'

'It sounds too melodramatic to me,' Kurma said. 'Are you sure you are not making it all up, Hathi dear?'

'It frightens the life out of me,' Chuhi squeaked, running up to sit alongside Lil Squi.

'I'm really, really scared.' said Lil Squi, who looked it.

'Ditto here,' Manu said.

'Even if it was half as true, we are all done for. Goners all,' Loombar said, his silver tongue beginning to lose its lustre rather rapidly.

'We will either drown or be crushed by falling trees,' Khargosh said.

'Or be swallowed by yawning cracks in Mother Earth. Horror of horrors.' Loombar could see himself falling down a bottomless crack in the earth.

'Eh, Mother Earth?' Kurma said, crossly. 'What sort of mother would do such a thing to her children?'

'What do we do then? What can we do?' The usually resourceful Manu felt utterly helpless. He went and sat on Hathi's back ,which was vaguely fortifying.

'We can pray for a miracle,' Lil Squi said.

'They say prayer can move mountains,' Chuhi said.

'We don't want mountains moved today, Chuhi,' Kurma said. 'We only want the earth not to move. That will do nicely.'

'If it is a minor quake, we'll be all right. If it is a major one, then God help us. By the ants' speed of flight, it doesn't seem it will be the former.' Hathi was not being an alarmist, he was merely being pragmatic. He wanted everybody to know the true colours of the picture they were about to see.

'What if you and your ants prove to be totally wrong, Hathi?' Kurma said.

'LOOK! LOOK! LOOK!' Hathi howled, pointing his trunk towards a curvaceous line in the grass which was rippling away in a great hurry. 'Ananta! He also knows because he too lives underground. Ananta! Ananta!' Hathi called out. 'Come join us. Let's see this thing through together.'

Ananta joined them, filling the peaceful glade with waves of nervous tension – Rajah and Ananta at the same place at the same time!

But old Hathi took matters in hand and set things right. 'When an earthquake strikes, there are no kings and no enemies. Like what we will be when we are before God.'

It became clear to one and all that the situation was serious, very, very, serious; otherwise Ananta would not have come to be here alongside Rajah. Never.

'Those wretched ants,' Kurma said. He withdrew his head into his shell and began to ponder the possibility of all that happening after all. How would this so-called earthquake affect him? His shell was strong. But it was not that strong – what if a boulder fell on him? He would be pulverized. The thought made Kurma shudder.

'Be thankful to the *kidis* for the warning,' Hathi said.

'Is it the end, then?' Mohan said. He had been quiet all this time, unable to understand any of it. 'Armageddon, as the human beings call this sort of thing?'

'At least we know what's coming. Imagine the men in their cities, towns and villages. They have no idea in spite of all their cleverness,' Hathi said.

'What will happen to them?' Manu asked.

'Their houses will crumble. Thousands will perish, crushed under falling buildings...'

'Oh, please, don't go on about it. I can't take it any more,' Mohan pleaded.

'But we are safe where we are, aren't we?' Rajah said, looking worried for the first time in his life. 'The trees are well away and it is hardly likely that the earth would open up right here, under our very feet.'

'How long will the quake last? One hour, two hours?' Cheetal, who had stood around, paralysed, as it were, by the deeply depressing prognostications, managed to open his mouth at last.

'A mere minute or two only. But you never can tell, Cheetal,' Ananta said. 'At the first tremor, lie down flat on the ground. You'll hear the earth's rumbles and you'll see trees collapse around you. Better, shut your eyes so you see nothing. But don't move and don't panic.'

'Panchchi Loag in the sky will be the safest. Wish we could fly as far as they can,' Mohan said, looking at Mohini.

'This reminds me,' Ananta went on. 'Minutes before the quake strikes, Panchchi Loag in the trees will take to the sky. They have a faultless instinct about it like the ants and us dwellers of the underworld.'

'Clearly, the end is near then. Can I make a last wish?' Mohan said.

'Take heart, Beautifullestest. You are not going to die, for heaven's sake.'

'But it feels as if I am going to and therefore I would like to make a last wish.'

'All right then, make it. And make it snappy,' Rajah said.

Thereupon, Mohan did something astonishing. He spread his magic circle around him and turned to Mohini: 'Will you marry me, Mademoiselle?'

While everybody present rolled their eyes in utter amazement at the timing of his proposal, Mohini was thrown in utter confusion.

'Now what shall I say?' whispered Mohini. And that was all she could manage.

'Say yes, say yes! And be done with it,' chorused all present. 'An earthquake is on his way, for heaven's sake.'

'Yes,' Mohini said, looking in Mohan's eyes.

Then Mohan addressed Rajah, 'Majesty, will you marry us?'

Now it was Rajah's turn to be taken aback.

'I am your King, not your priest and confessor,' he said, indignantly.

'Sire,' Hathi saved the situation, 'in certain countries the King is also the High Priest.'

Rajah turned to Ananta for advice. This was the first time in his entire life that the tiger had spoken to the cobra, surprising every junglebody, surprising the great serpent and most of all, himself.

'Ananta, what do you say? You are also a King, King of the Underworld.'

'I would marry them, Rajah.'

'Even though they are about to perish, Ananta?'

'I hope they don't. I hope none of us does. But this makes it all the more necessary that you wed them, Rajah.'

'All right then. Come here, you two.'

Their eyes in each other's, Mohan and Mohini tip-toed to the centre of the gathering, making as handsome a couple as any that ever walked the earth.

'I suppose you need a witness, don't you? Choose one and hurry. We haven't got all day.'

'Ananta, would you do the honours?' Mohan said.

'With great pleasure.'

'There, you have a royal witness,' Rajah said.

'Royalty to wed, royalty to witness! My word!' Kurma said, popping his neck out and opening his eyes wide.

'Kurma, cut it out. Not the time for your quips.'

'Sorry, Majesty. Sorry.'

Rajah then spoke solemnly: 'Do you, Mohan, the self-appointed Beautifullestest, take the truly Beautifullestest Mohini as your lawful wedded wife?'

'I do.'

'And you, Mohini, do you do vice versa?'

'I do.'

'There. I pronounce you Peacock and Peahen. Phew!'

Those were delicious words to the ears of the groom. But no sooner had they been uttered, Panchchi Loag in the trees shot to the sky, as if a bad man had fired a gun!

'LIE DOWN! LIE DOWN!,' howled Hathi.

The earth first rumbled, then it moved and after that it simply turned upside down. Great trees came crashing to the ground noisily and the river rose like a wall of water. Then it spilled over, flooding the jungle. The earth trembled yet again, making an almighty din and frightening all prostrate junglebodies. The earth quaked a third time, bringing down more trees. The earth moved for the last time and much of the river water ran back into the river.

Then it was all over.

Only silence, except for the hysterical chatter of the Panchchi Loag in the sky.

Gradually, in spite of the catastrophe, the usual jungle noises came alive. Frogs croaked, the crickets screeched and the Panchchi Loag began to squabble among themselves, now from the trees.

And Rajah roared as he laboured to get out of a long ditch of flood water.

'I hate earthquakes. I hate earthquakes.'

'Having a hard time, Majesty?' teased Manu from the one tree which had been left standing nearby.

'Cheeky monkey! Sarcasm is the lowest form of wit. I told you once and I'm telling you again. So...?'

'Only a friendly remark, Majesty. Have a sense of humour.'

'Humour? Humour?' grumbled Rajah. 'No such thing as humour in an earthquake.'

'But the quake is over. So rejoice.'

'Rejoice? Sometimes I simply do not understand you, Manu.'

A little later, the jungle met for a headcount. Nobody was missing, only the newlyweds.

'Honeymoon? Earthquake honeymoon? Earth-moving honeymoon!' Kurma sang impishly.

'Kurma, what I like about you is your timing, never saying the wrong thing at the wrong time,' Manu said. 'Don't you think, Majesty?'

Was Rajah listening? He was too preoccupied with what the earthquake had done to his jungle. He blamed it on Hathi.

'Look what it has done. How many trees it has felled.'

'New trees will grow where the old ones have fallen. It's Mother Nature, Sire.'

'I hope you are right.'

Rajah and Hathi stood by a small pool made by the tilting of the river, its water calm and still. Rajah happened to look into its mirror-like surface. He saw those eyes that set jungle nights ablaze, and those awesome stripes – over which Chanda Mama glanced adoringly – rippled as a gust of breeze breathed over the pool. Rajah liked what he saw. And the sun-soaked magic of an afternoon, eerily quiet after the great earthly upheaval, also liked what it saw – a vision of immaculate perfection. Rajah issued a muffled roar of satisfaction and walked with matchless grace away into the glittering gold.

The End

This edition published in 2010 by
Mapin Publishing Pvt. Ltd
502 Paritosh, Near Darpana Academy
Usmanpura Riverside
Ahmedabad 380013 INDIA
T: 91 79 402 28 228 | F: 91 79 402 28 201
E: mapin@mapinpub.com | www.mapinpub.com

Simultaneously published in the
United States of America by
Grantha Corporation
77 Daniele Drive, Hidden Meadows
Ocean Township, NJ 07712
E: mapin@mapinpub.com

First published in India in 2009 by
Mapin Publishing
in association with
HarperCollins *Children's* Books, an imprint of
HarperCollins *Publishers* India

Illustrations by Sean Victory

ISBN: 978-81-89995-05-8 (Mapin) pb
ISBN: 978-81-89995-56-0 (Mapin) hc
ISBN: 978-1-935677-03-1 (Grantha)
LCCN: 2010932787

Designed by Gopal Limbad / Mapin Design Studio
Edited by Diana Romany / Mapin Editorial

Printed in India by EIH Limited-Unit Press